Second thoughts from a GRUMPY innovator

written & illustrated by costas papaikonomou

Copyright ©2015 Costas Papaikonomou

All rights reserved. No part of this book may be reproduced in any form or by any electronic or mechanical means including information storage and retrieval systems, without permission in writing from the author.

This is the first edition, June 2015

Twitter: @grumpyinnovator
Email: costas@grumpyinnovator.com
Web: grumpyinnovator.com

ISBN 979-868-383-3749

*to Patricia, Spiro and Dimi
my anti-grumpidotes.*

[**The future isn't in front of you, but *behind* you. Merciless in pursuit, on your heels, preying on every last decision you made, awaiting your next move.**]

Second Thoughts

In 2012, I published the first Grumpy Innovator book about the ugly reality of innovation in corporate environments and the responses have been heart-warming;

- "Thank god I am not alone, I thought I was the crazy one here at the office."
- "I read a few lines every time I'm in the toilet. I've found it a great inspiration and laxative."
- "It made me laugh and then cry when I realised I was the topic of the joke myself."
- "It made me cry in the toilet at the office, thank god I was alone at the time."

Three years later, there is good news and bad news.

The good news is that the book has put me in touch with countless new friends, who share my amazement of how organisations deal with innovation and get in trouble when they need to do doing things differently in order to grow, or even survive. There is an army of us out there, who will patiently sit through long meetings and tedious processes, waiting for the right moment to do what we know is required to actually get things done.

The bad news is we're still a minority and I'm still grumpy. Which is why you're now holding this second book: I've had no problem finding more stuff to write about.

Scattered across these pages you will find further thoughts on reasons why innovation is still a painful activity for so many businesses.

Premise: why I'm still grumpy	6
Which mouths do I put my money in?	13
Murky Mechanics Of Innovation	39
Build The Brand & Own The Copy	64
Tail Wag Dog	85
Luck, Patience & Being Right	114

Premise: why I'm still grumpy

In the first Grumpy Innovator book I explored the paradox of innovation[1]. The conflict between a messy, ever-changing outside world which drives the need to innovate, versus wanting a predictable, calm environment in which it is easier to run a profitable business. In corporate ecosystems, this leads to over-relying on models and abstract views of the world, resulting in poor success rates. It was also fun to throw rocks at various functions who we all know get in the way of things more than anything.

What I'd like to explore with you in this second book is a number of perspectives on 'innovation' itself. What is it, how does it strain people & processes and what core competencies does a business need to do it well? But most of all to throw a couple more rocks and have some fun.

On the next two pages is a diagram showing the Sunny Smile of Innovation alongside its dark mirror image, the Murky Mechanics of Innovation. We'll explore how innovation is more than the business textbook definition of 'doing something new that makes money' or 'drives growth'. It comes in different shades and cannot be seen without its implications on the organisation delivering it.

---

[1] *You can find the first book's premise on page 146*

Sunny Smile Of Innovation

Innovation is a commercial tool for businesses to continuously seek out new revenue opportunities, and

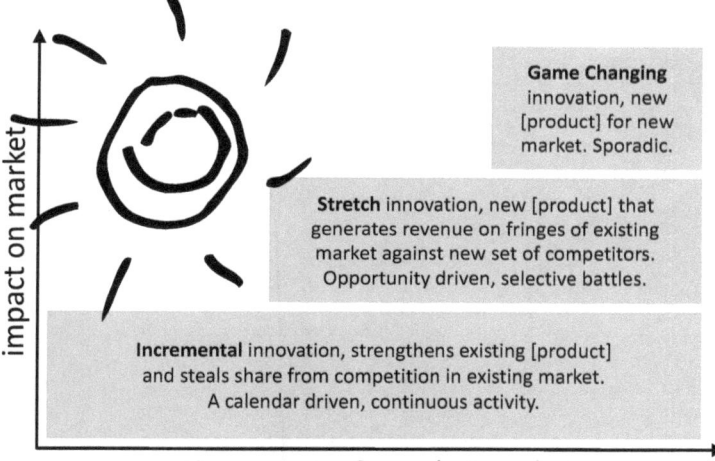

(chart: impact on market vs. time passes & market evolves)

Game Changing innovation, new [product] for new market. Sporadic.

Stretch innovation, new [product] that generates revenue on fringes of existing market against new set of competitors. Opportunity driven, selective battles.

Incremental innovation, strengthens existing [product] and steals share from competition in existing market. A calendar driven, continuous activity.

that's the bright happy side shown here.

- **Incremental**: this is your 'new news' process. Small tweaks to satisfy new questions from existing users/clients and piss off competition.
- **Stretch**: find new occasions and formats to draw in an audience just beyond your current reach. Great if you're starting to lose on price in your current market and things are commoditizing.
- **Game Changers**: The sexy end of the spectrum, where you create a lasting legacy, get your face on magazine covers and re-invent the industry.

Murky Mechanics Of Innovation

When most business books and creative gurus talk about 'disruption', they refer to messing up your competitors' heads and shaking up the market.

(chart: impact on organisation vs. time & resource requirements)

Incremental, change settings in the factory & update sales team. **6-18 Months.**

Stretch, find gap with new target audience, get R&D to develop new [product], order new lines in factory, train sales team and build relationships with new buyers. **A year or two?**

Game Changing, as Stretch *plus* develop new technical capabilities & IP, create new business model, build new factory, find new suppliers, replace personnel by new team with right skill set, create new distribution, ditch existing portfolio & its revenue stream. **OMFG Kill Me.**

That's *not* it. You are disrupting yourself much more.

- **Incremental**: a cross-functional effort you can tightly plan and control, within set ecosystems.
- **Stretch**: Requires understanding new category consumers and business rules, creation of minor new capability and your best bet for growing your market when you're still calling the shots.
- **Game Changers**: Only when your back is against the wall, your current [product] is completely commoditized or the market is going extinct.

2nd grumpy innovator

So what does this dark and disheartening mirror image mean? It shows that not only do you need particular functions inside your business to innovate pragmatically in a messy world to keep the machines running[2], you also need an additional set of meta-capabilities to adapt your organisation as much as the market you're serving;

- The ability to share responsibility for innovation across functions; in parallel, not sequentially, with the lead switching sensibly as the work progresses. Similarly, realising that the source of the opportunity can come from anywhere too – sales, technology, distribution, etcetera – *not* just consumer focus groups and market research.
- Acute awareness of the required impact your innovation needs to make in order to achieve your business objective. Create an incremental innovation when that'll do the job, reserve game changers for when you need (or can afford) one.
- Savvy use of expensive assets over time, retaining function and relevance beyond the initially intended launch products and support future revenue as well.
- Install processes across the business functions that drive for value-add to the end result, your product. Not solely to optimize operational efficiency. It is the simplest way to ensure you keep aiming for relevancy *and* pick up early signals of change right at the source: the customers of your products and services.
- Acknowledgment that when you move up into Stretch and Game Changing innovation, you are also moving *away* from daily procedures and into new ball games with unknown rules. That means success will depend more than anything on the judgment of the people

---

[2] *See first Grumpy Innovator book*

creating the innovation, not on prescribed ways of working. *Trust* them.

I'll share my grumpy thoughts on pitfalls on these five principles, along with ways that might make life just a little easier. Might. A little.

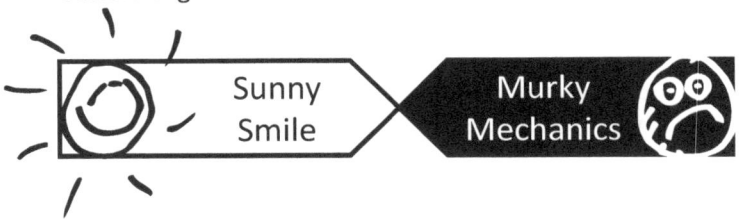

Sunny Smile → Murky Mechanics

You may now be thinking... wait a moment, aren't today's celebrated new heroes of innovation in the digital arena doing all that Game Changing in the blink of an eye *and* making a fortune on the go?

Yes – *and*.

Putting those new digital heroes in a more realistic and perhaps even cynical perspective;

- The vast majority of the global economy runs on businesses who *make* things, not on digital platforms for selling or accessing them. This will remain the case in our lifetime, at least as long as humans consume physical foods & goods.
- Most, if not *all* billion-dollar start-ups prove to be pyramid schemes, not making any profitable revenue stream, ever. Then they collapse.
- The digital space is big and sexy, but it's also an immature Wild West in comparison to say, laundry detergents, chewing gum or dry soups.

This book is for people who are in the business of making and selling real things, to highly competitive mass markets around the globe. People building brands by carefully crafting relevant improvements to win their consumers' hearts. For them, the Murky Mechanics Of Innovation are a reality that tires them by day and keeps them awake at night.

I salute you.

Costas Papaikonomou
June 2015

2nd grumpy innovator

Which mouths do I put my money in?

**THE FINANCE TEAM IS PRETTY SURE
THIS IS WHAT OUR CONSUMERS WANT.**

Which mouths do I put my money in?

Somewhere, early autumn: a cross-functional discussion in a corporate meeting room.

CEO: *Knocks on table with toy hammer.*
"My dearest Innovation Committee, that was a good start. Now let's move on to agenda item 2. By the way, who's taking notes today? Anyway – ahem – agenda item 2 is to allocate our innovation budgets for the next 5 years. I have 10 million cash-thingies reserved. What do you think?"

R&D: "Well, that depends. It's ₡3m more than we had last year before you came on board. Which is great, as we overspent ₡2m this year on catching up with [competitor]. But it was worth it as we are now ready to file patents of our own and won't need to work with [supplier] anymore."

Finance: "Did you budget for filing patents? That's expensive."

R&D: *Ruffles papers.*
"Well, that depends. We did for US & Europe, but Sales wants to ship [product] to Asia."

Finance: "So that's a No."
Scribbles in notepad, with stern face.

Marketing: "Sorry I'm late. What are we discussing today?"

CEO: "Innovation budgets for the next 5 years. And late arrivals get note-taking duty. We just started and R&D is asking for ₡2m to plug last year's gap."

Marketing: "We need to change that notes rule, it's unfair to busy people. But good to hear we're talking innovation. I need a game changer next year. After that I don't know yet. How much does a game changer cost?"

2nd grumpy innovator

R&D: "Well, that depends. Do you have a spec?"

Marketing: "No, I'm waiting for the U&A to come in."

Market Research: "Preliminary U&A findings are due in 3 months."

Marketing: "Hey, I hadn't seen you were here. Hi. But wait, you said 3 months at last month's meeting too."

Market Research: "Yes, and then you all-of-a-sudden urgently wanted to include Asia, while fieldwork in Europe and North America had already started. And don't look at me like that."
Rolls eyes.

Marketing: "Ya Ya. Touché. Anyway, without a spec, how much does a game changer cost? Ball-park will do."

R&D: "Well, that depends. Last year's [game changer] was only ₡5m but it did take 4 years to develop. Do you want to know what we can do in 1 year or do you want a game changer?"

Marketing: "I'm not sure I understand but either way, I can't spec without the U&A and I do need something next year."

Manufacturing: *Raises finger.*
"Sorry, can I say something?"

Marketing: "Maybe you can work from the segmentation? The infographics are really inspiring and it's pretty accurate except for France."

Sales: "Hey hold on, France just happens to be the only market that consistently makes the numbers. Remember who's paying the salaries here. We are."

CEO: "Guys, just a second. Manufacturing would like to say something."

Manufacturing: "Thank you. Well, I just wanted to say 3 of our 4 plants are severely underutilized already, since the orders for

	the last [game changer] have been disappointing. If we scrap all that kit now, we won't hit the ROI we promised."
CEO:	"OK, that's a clear message. I suggest we forget about the game changers for next year and ensure we utilize our factories a bit better first. We have shareholder value to protect. The Six Sigma team are on the case, no?"
Manufacturing:	"Plants. They're called plants, not factories. And the Six Sigma guys have indeed optimized the lines such we can make [game changer] more effectively, but we haven't anything new to fill the excess capacity so we're now nearing 30% idle."
CEO:	"Sorry, plants. Not factories. Whatever. But are you saying TQM has made our plants more effective or less effective? I'm confused now."
Sales:	"Hey hold on. You're changing the subject. How do I beat off [competitor product] if I can barely offer parity with [our product], even when I cut out all the margin? What do we do about that first?"
R&D:	"Well, that depends. We could go back in time, properly spec it and then design it cheaper, faster and better. Shall we do that? Oh no – DUH – time travel hasn't been invented yet."
Marketing:	"Ya Ya. Spare me the sarcasm. Our whole marketing team was different 2 years ago, how could *they* know what *we* would want to work on, eh? Besides, I want a game changer because I have a brand to build. I'll cut the comms budget to fund new kit in the factory if I need to."
Finance:	"You'll do what? Cash-thingies cannot be moved around like that. Comms, factories, we need to follow the process, ISO audit season is coming."

2nd grumpy innovator

Manufacturing: "They're called *plants*, please. And that's exactly how we funded the new lines 4, 6, 11 and 14 years ago. I know because I was there every time to sign the paperwork."

CEO: *Knocks toy hammer on table again.*
"This is going nowhere. I asked a simple question at the beginning. How do we spend our ₡10m over the next 5 years? We need to innovate because that's what well run businesses do. Fewer Bigger Better.
Who owns the Innovation Funnel? I mean the Stage Gate"

All: "Market Research!" / "M&D/eting!"

CEO: "What?"

Manufacturing: "Well, Supply Chain write all the contracts for anything new we do. But they're not part of this Innovation Committee. They're the only people *we* deal with when sorting out capacity, suppliers or anything new and that's been working fine for twenty years."

Market Research: "Ha! Well, we're a consumer centric company now and they don't represent our consumer. That time is behind us. Market Research should own the innovation funnel because *we* are the Voice Of The Consumer."

R&D: "You mean you put every single one of my team's ideas in front of your focus groups. That's where most of my overspend went."

CEO: *Hammers more loudly now.*
"Jeez, settle down guys. Last time I checked, Procurement is part of Supply Chain and since we initiated the PartnersPlus programme, they control what market research we buy too. Now, can someone make a note to invite Supply Chain at next month's meeting to present the Innovation Funnel or Stage Gate or whatever it is they do to chart how we spend innovation budgets around here?
Now, who's making notes?"

Hopefully, you recognize nothing whatsoever of that scene and you have the innovation responsibilities clearly defined in your organization. Then the problem of budgeting for the future becomes as simple as: how much do I spend on what and when?

The problem with innovation resource is of course it's about planning for unknown solutions to yet uncertain problems and the further out in time you look the worse it gets. The only thing certain is it will be expensive, and there's never enough cash. The business books talk about building a car while driving it, but none mention the blinking fuel indicator.

Then how place your bets, when it comes to innovation investments? Is it about bringing the trend watchers in and watching them perform their 2×2 magic on flipcharts? Is it about sinking money in local start-ups hoping for a return? Or simply spend it on 10% free-wheeling time for your technical teams?

The problem of course, is the immensely different time lines that your technical and marketing teams operate on. Ask your R&D team how long it takes to develop a particular capability and the default answer is 5 years, plus a request for an expensive piece of laboratory kit. Ask your marketing team what new products they expect to need in 5 years' time and they'll tell you what they think they might need next year, along with a massive market research budget.

In essence, both teams are right. In the myopic world of foresight, they're saying the same thing: "We don't know how the future will affect us". Which is useless if you need to decide now where to invest for long term capabilities, be it technical or operational.

The answer lies in de-constructing this huge question into smaller chunks *and* the simple ambition to shape the future instead of just trying to guess what might happen. Remarkable opportunities reveal themselves when you look at the future through different lenses for things you can do;

- **Consumer & society**. What's going on in the lives of your end-consumer, throughout the day? How do the different generations use your products and what does that say about their next life stage?
- **Technology**. What are barriers you and your competitors are all running into, the contradictions and trade-offs that come with delivering your core benefit?
- **Channel & distribution**. How are the channels you are in now evolving? How do you make those even easier for your products to run through? What new channels are emerging?
- **Point of sale**. Will your end-users be buying products from you at the same point in time and place, or is this likely to change? Same for your middleman or retailer.
- **Environment & supply chain**. How can environmental impact be reduced, not just for ethical reasons, but also to overcome rising scarcity of just about every raw ingredient known to man?
- **Legal**. What does the regulatory landscape look like, what new rules and limitations are likely to be imposed on you? Look at categories that might serve as ominous precedents.
- **Brand**. If you were to just extrapolate what your brands have been doing so far, what would the effect be of multiplying by ten times faster, softer, harder, smoother, nicer …?

Etcetera. Defining the right set of lenses is *not* an exact science[3], the trick is to cast a wide net of relevant yet distinctly different directions that matter for your business.

Explore future scenarios first, through each of your lenses. Go further out than you'd ever be comfortable with for ROI calculations, it's OK. Have your technical and commercial teams spend some quality time together on thinking up what *the world* will look like in 5 to 10 years' time, not what they will be doing themselves. How will these changes affect your industry, your category, your markets. Ideate for 15-20 product/service concepts that would do well in your future world.

>>> PAUSE FOR SIDE STEP:

If you're struggling to go beyond the obvious, use this simple old Soviet[4] trick. In the future, everything becomes more ideal at delivering its core benefit:

1. **Perfectly,** at optimal impact, sweetness, delight and efficacy.
2. **Instantly,** only when and where necessary.
3. **Autonomously,** with no material nor info required from the beneficiary.
4. **Free** to the recipient.

Just think about it - if any competitor would introduce something that surpasses you on one of those four dimensions, you're in trouble. If they hit 2 or more - you're **toast** - and you don't need a single focus group nor technology scan to figure that out. But you will need to be clear on

---

[3] *In fact, people stating that looking into the future is a science with any degree of certainty, have no more accuracy than a horoscope. Anyone with actual certainty about the future would not be telling nor selling it to you, but using that information to make bazillions in the stock market.*
There are no trend agencies in the Fortune500 last time I checked.

[4] *TRIZ – go check Wikipedia. It's the closest you'll get to objective problem solving.*

> what your core benefit actually is as it might
> not be what you think. For example, if you're in
> the business of lawnmowers: the ideal isn't an
> autonomous robo-mower, nor ceramic blades, nor
> solar power. Because the core benefit that people
> want is nice lawns, the ideal result is more
> likely to be self-cutting grass. Which means your
> future might lie crop genetics which is a
> completely different industry from garden
> machinery.
>
> Shaping the Future implies tackling category
> barriers.
>
> <<< END OF SIDE STEP.

Chart & rank what technical capabilities you'd need to create your concepts for a future world. For every one of your future concepts, list a maximum of 3 new capabilities you would need to have matured in order to deliver them profitably. Again, go 360: review technology, supply chain, sourcing, distribution and so on. Not the functional teams in your business, but the capabilities you'd need to develop if you were a start-up. Chart the overlap between them across concepts. Which capabilities appear over and over, as critical for multiple concepts? You're getting warmer now, most likely a top-5 of core capabilities is emerging: the platforms that will give you most bang for buck wherever the future winners turn out to be.

Review their implications, and then some more. This is where it gets fun. For each of the key capabilities, list the implications across your business (internal) and market (external) of implementing them. Then list the implications of those implications. You'll be surprised at what that second round reveals. Most likely, your list of core capabilities halved along the way, and at least one new joiner appeared.

Ask yourself what you need just to play the game and where you can excel to win? This automatically takes you into 'make or buy' considerations. This last step is surprisingly easy and shamefully often overlooked. Practice saying "MAKE or BUY?" out loud in front of a mirror, and then in front of your technical team, it will turn heads. For some reason, too many organizations culturally assume everything needs to be developed from scratch. Look again at your shortlist of capabilities you need in order to thrive in the future, in the context of what passed in all three steps before. Which of them are actually mere nice-to-haves, platform standards that most likely already exist in other industries? Just BUY them, now. Then ask yourself what are the ownable, differentiating capabilities you want to excel at and win? MAKE them or buy the companies that make them. Start developing and patenting like there is no tomorrow. Because there is.

Are you awaiting the future, or shaping it?

Charting innovation bets and deciding where to invest your innovation budget becomes much easier once you realize you don't need 20-20 vision on what the future will bring, nor spreading the bet across a huge number of alternatives. As long as you know what you need to be good at.

> **Innovation success is mostly about luck, and resisting the temptation to gamble.**

2nd grumpy innovator

"Stop being so stressed" - the single most useless advice you can receive when you're stressed.

Most Marketers talk with their Manufacturing team just like they talk to the guy in the blue overall who repairs their car. Fearful & impatient.

If you're considering developing complicated products for Millennials, be aware that by the time you launch they'll be nearing 40.

Everything so far in your career is a consequence of your own choices. So is everything from here on.

Innovative destruction and hopelessness: long queues for collecting benefits. By that I mean marketers lining up for focus groups.

"I had a beer, please"
A futurologist walks into a bar

Hey Marketer, if you want your CEO to suck up every opinion you ventilate, pre-empt it by "we've been hearing in focus groups that..."

Consumer centricity =
[time spent convincing consumers] /
[time spent convincing internal stakeholders].
Try scoring > 1%

> **Love as marketing concept statement:**
> *You're lonely & need love*
> *Discover Me*
> *You'll feel super amazing*
> *Because only I give TLC*
> *Me Me Me*

Success in market is less dependent on the perfect idea, than it being an idea a small team is willing to work overtime for to improve and make a reality.

Time for my legal team meeting to discuss our new claims strategy!
Packs wooden stakes, crucifixes and garlic.

"We will do focus groups to let our consumers define our strategy", he said, followed by the hissing sound of all hope deflating into a vacuum.

"Fewer & Bigger Innovation" also implies "Less Innovations". Which means the required competence isn't scaling but the ability to choose.

To pessimists, the glass is half empty.
Meanwhile, the optimists are making a mess and splashing water all over themselves.

2nd grumpy innovator

**COVERING YOUR ARSE IN PILES OF RESEARCH
JUST MAKES IT LOOK BIGGER.**

A management culture of looking down the hierarchy for answers ("you tell me what to choose") is passed down all the way to the focus group.

"We have an informal, flat organisation", said the Secretary General.

Millennials, temper your heroic expectations.
Actual things you do before you die: sore joints, dementia, kidney stones & maybe cough blood.

A framework for "judging quality" isn't meant for "creating quality", ie. reviewers are not the makers. In business that is misunderstood.

Navigating your innovation project through murky C-Suite waters will likely involve more coochy-coochy with your CFO than your CEO or CMO.

> **"I can change him!"**
> *Women attracted to the wrong men*
> *and marketers trying to attract consumers.*

Nature's fundamental Weak, Strong, Electro-Magnetic and Gravity forces ... meet their corporate mirror Wimp, Ego, Internet and Guru forces.

Bulls and China shops. Sometimes it really is the China shop's fault.

Hey Boomers, the house with the big mortgage you're leaving as inheritance would be better named as 'tax bill', 'debt' or just 'no house'.

Buying stock of a business that's never made profit: gambling. Selling that stock on before it does make profit: pyramid scheme.

The fact you've overcome huge internal organisational hurdles to launch this product is irrelevant to the audience buying it, sorry.

> **Presume the opportunity needs to be MADE, not FOUND. It'll set you up better for the journey ahead.**

Rising into the middle classes brings two emotional drivers into the mix: "I hope I don't fall back" and
"I hope my kids do even better".

Remember that growth requires non-linear resources. 10% extra revenue might well eat up 80% more of your energy.

"Consumers always say the same things!"
Marketer ignorant of his/her products always having the same problems.

If you're not sure if the trending behaviour will continue, then plan for the other two options as well: stalling or reversing.

The biggest obstacle to getting lucky is presuming everything happens for a reason.

Charting future states without charting their implications for your business is like, well... useless.

If you want to see a stale team be creative, ask them to come up with reasons not to change anything. They'll have 100's of ideas.

"There is no life jacket underneath your seat. Nor seatbelts for when we hit turbulence. Parachutes, maybe." = Innovation reality.

Being able to see the merit of someone else's work and use it to complement or even replace your own, is a brave creative leap, not theft.

Someone probably already had that great idea of yours before you. Probably someone sitting in the same canteen as you every day.

The best way forward from your current position is making yourself obsolete. Simply because it forces you to move on and reinvent yourself.

I have a hunch that prosperity is roughly Bell-curve shaped. Not for income, but for the amount of trash you permit yourself to generate.

Arrogance: "I am right".
Confidence: "I can make it right, whatever happens".
Indifference: "Right, whatever".

If you create a clear distinction in your organisation between customer acquisition and retention, you will have equally disparate results.

I thought you did your 3-year plan last year?

Rank your own job's redundancy score:

$$\frac{[\text{"other functions would prefer to get stuff done without me"}]}{[\text{"who'd notice if they do"}]}$$

"Pfff. We can put a man on the moon but we can't get a live web stream to work"
IT nag overlooking we can no longer put a man on the moon.

"Has the potential to revolutionise [X]" and "Is revolutionising [X]" are two very different things, but continuously confused.

Hey leadership team, are you reading performance or assessing potential? Not the same.

Nothing distorts your view on the future more than what you perceive as your investments in the past. Your past self might have been wrong.

"The Schmeeting Point" - the point when more time is spent in meetings discussing what to do, than the time spent doing what is discussed.

$$\left[\textbf{Is your Innovation time line expressed in man-years or dog-years?} \right]$$

If Serendipity and Luck got the credit they deserved in business, there would be way less business books.

Water is a subset of coffee.

Almost everyone operates with best intent. That includes those b**tards you consider as barriers to your project success.

That unsettling moment you realize you can whistle along with the teleconference holding music and the robotic announcer sounds like an old friend.

If you're not sure it's going to annoy the hell out of your competitors, is it really worth the hassle?

I just learned a new word which I must use more often: "bifurcation". Wow.

"Less Is More". Try saying that to your shareholders with the same enthusiasm you're trying to convince your customers and suppliers.

Scoping or just coping?

The fact you disagree doesn't mean you're right.

Hey futurologist, technically you're not looking into THE future but A future. Note the subtle but important nuance there.

"It was one value-engineered step too many for me"
If consumers had the vocabulary to express why they turned their back on you.

The market research paradox. The more research you do, the more likely you are to hear/see conflicting things. Do it iteratively.

[**Roughly right is better than precisely wrong.**]

"We want to be as innovative as Apple." – Then you should make a plan to launch iTunes 10 years ago.

Isn't it about time to update quant survey Lickert scores to "LOL - OMG - LIKE - MEH - FFS - FML"...?

Being informed and being opinionated are not the same thing, either can be true without the other.

**PROTECT THE INTROVERT OPTIMIST
AND SHUN THE EXTROVERT PESSIMIST.**

If you keep your headphones on while asking me for directions, I will send you the wrong way, OK?

"Make Or Buy?"
The C-suite paradigm for innovation which too often defaults to "Make" and then fails.

> **Hey SVP, do your innovation teams spend more time preparing for meeting with you or with your consumers?**

Assumption is the mother of all disaster. But that's just an assumption, obviously.

"There's no downside to this opportunity, it's incredible!"
An opportunity with no up-side either.

> **In a shrinking market, copying your competition is probably not a smart thing to do.**

If you gather enough data, causality and correlation lose meaning as you can prove anything you want.

"Robust forecasting procedures" is an oxymoron.
If your system requires a lot of forecasting to run smoothly, it is clearly very fragile.

A: "The shame & blame culture in this organisation is absolutely horrendous!"
B: "We need to find who's causing it and fire them!"

There's no dreaming during sleepless nights.

The goalposts aren't moving, the field is.

Saying innovation is only about finding the right idea, is like saying you can keep an alligator's mouth shut with one hand and not bother about the other 15ft.

Half my fellow grads from 20 years ago now work in industries that didn't exist when we graduated. Makes you wonder what universities are supposed to teach.

If you're using macro trends to inform your innovation strategy, you're probably forgetting how micro your share-of-wallet really is.

It seems a lot of lifestyle businesses fear missing out on the Fear Of Missing Out trend.

A: "Let's ask a couple of total strangers for sign-off on our strategy."
B: "No f-ing way."
A: "Let's do focus groups then."
B: "Yes!"

The buck usually stops over there.

Judging by this stack of MR reports I've just scanned, Women's Lib must have happened in a parallel reality.
It's all "Clean-Feed-Care-Repeat"...?

Mental note for next year's planning cycle: 'Hope' is not a strategy.

Creating, developing and launching in 8 months is pointless if you start 5 years too late.

"Women and children first!"
Marketing

"Not Invented Here" is absolutely fine as long as it's not being "Invented Over There" either.

"Reframing" aka "Deja New"

"Hold that thought!"
A guarantee to forget that thought. WRITE IT DOWN.

If you are category leader, then you shouldn't be awaiting the future, but shaping it. Actually, you should do that whatever share you have.

"What's the benefit of doing this?" versus "What's the cost of doing nothing?"
Short term versus long term views.

Sorry for my ignorance, but which of your MBA courses taught you "coupons" as strategy device?
Or was it as an intrinsic value multiplier?

In debate with R&D team looking for tools to save money on prototypes and need your help: where can I order a ruler with a half measures scale?

Inertia is not an external factor stopping you. Neither is paralysis.

"My predecessor was excellent and I have no plans to change the strategy, at least not for a while"
No one in management, ever

Innovation road map: Ask directions (*without shame*) / Straight on (*probably not*) / Correct course (*all the time*) / U-turn (*last resort*).

When dealing with ambiguous alternatives to choose from, it's less about what you choose & more about how well you stick to what you chose.

If you have to resort to crowd sourcing to find your company's next big idea, then you're not really in control of its future are you?

"Fifty Shades Of Orange" – A saucy new bestseller on interpreting mixed results from quant research.

If you're wondering what the CEO of 2030 will be like, don't ask today's CEOs to predict. Talk to the stars in today's middle management.

If you want to get senior stakeholders on board, make it sound like you're letting them in on a secret. Being covert beats being loud.

If you need over a year to sign off a foresight project, it has become an insight project. Another year, and it's a post-mortem project....

"Stage gate process" anagrams to "Sage protects sage", which then anagrams to "Greets scapegoats". *Remember, you read it here first.*

"Hidden development projects are no longer possible in our business, we have full transparency"
Someone unaware why 'hidden' is called 'hidden'.

We (*I*) made a unanimous (*polarising*) decision (*compromise*) based on observations (*hearsay*), facts (*opinions*) and foresight (*hindsight*).

"Business Analyst" anagrams to "An Unstable Sissy".

To explain your junior team member what to listen out for in focus groups, just say "WhatsApp me all the WTFs & LOLs".

Just to check, when was the last time you used one of your own products?

Few things are black & white in innovation, except for this: you MUST be comfortable with ambiguity.

$\Big[$ **Don't be fooled by political barriers being introduced as technical barriers.** $\Big]$

Solutionocracy: the deification of people good at suggesting solutions, even when there aren't any problems.

*** SPOILER ALERT ***
Consumers have no idea what 'category' means, nor which one your brand/product belongs to.

Sadly, many global businesses seem to think that Developing Markets can be satisfied with Under-Developed Products.

Do not complain about your boss' inability to think long term if you've covered yourself in tattoos.

"Level five corporate leadership" anagrams to "Verified poser, all over the place". Remember, you read it here first.

Your number of options seldom decrease over time. They just increase in cost the longer you wait.

AS THE GERMANS SAY, A "WURST KÄSE" SCENARIO

The real-old Polaroids of Me versus the fake-old Instagrams of Me ... the Polaroid-Me looks real-young and the Instagram-Me real-old.

Wisdom Of Crowds: "Faster Horses"
Wisdom Of Operations: "Cheaper Horses"
Wisdom Of R&D: "Smarter Horses"
Wisdom Of Marketers: "New Size! Ponies!"

[Are things really getting better or have you merely revised your expectations?]

2nd grumpy innovator

Murky Mechanics Of Innovation

**WHAT DO YOU MEAN?
THIS *IS* THE WHOLE PORTFOLIO.**

Murky Mechanics Of Innovation

Paraphrasing Albert Einstein;

> "Only a moron will believe that going through the same process twice will deliver a different result."

That paradox sits at the core of creating processes for embedding an innovation culture and capability into any corporation. It's real friction;

- Businesses want predictable innovation processes that deliver on the clock, at budget.
- Innovation is meant to retain relevance and deliver to a mostly unpredictable outside world.

How to navigate that gap? How come some businesses out there manage to pump out new products successfully year-after-year with process excellence and others fail miserably?

This is about balancing the Sunny Smile and Murky Mechanics Of Innovation.

The answer lies in understanding the different degrees of innovation impact. Too often, innovation is regarded merely as making money from new things for customers and consumers. What is overlooked, is the impact those new things have on the business itself.

2nd grumpy innovator

impact on market

Game Changing innovation, new [product] for new market. Sporadic.

Stretch innovation, new [product] that generates revenue on fringes of existing market against new set of competitors. Opportunity driven, selective battles.

Incremental innovation, strengthens existing [product] and steals share from competition in existing market. A calendar driven, continuous activity.

impact on organisation

Incremental, change settings in the factory & update sales team. **6-18 Months.**

Stretch, find gap with new target audience, get R&D to develop new [product], order new lines in factory, train sales team and build relationships with new buyers. **A year or two?**

Game Changing, as Stretch *plus* develop new technical capabilities & IP, create new business model, build new factory, find new suppliers, replace personnel by new team with right skill set, create new distribution, ditch existing portfolio & its revenue stream. **OMFG Kill Me.**

Let's Look at these in a little more detail …

Sunny Smile Of <u>INCREMENTAL</u>

Innovation to strengthen your proposition and deliver 'new news' along only one dimension, e.g. product. Most, if not all other dimensions remain the same. So you know who you're selling to, through which channels, at what price. You're innovating to steal share in well-defined market. You are probably already well equipped to roll-out these new products.

Because this is all about evolving minor tweaks within well-defined parameters, this type of innovation can be honed to a calendar-driven process excellence, delivering new products to market like clockwork.

But most importantly, you are doing this *all the time*, to maintain relevance to your consumers and please your middle-man buyers. From the moment you launch your product, you start lining up regular (small) improvements to keep copycats and competitors behind you. Ending only when the category goes extinct.

Another benefit of installing a good system for incremental innovation is that it's a great training ground for young innovators of all functions to cut their teeth, one dimension at a time.

Murky Mechanics Of <u>INCREMENTAL</u>

At first glance, you wouldn't expect too many issues here. It's controllable, relatively quick and low risk.

Yet herein lies the danger – because this is in effect 'innovation for innovation's sake', one can be tricked into thinking it's enough just to be *different*. It isn't, you still need to find improvements that are relevant to your audience.

Even trickier is when the process excellence team comes in, because they'll have a cost optimisation agenda to push. Not that there's anything wrong with trying to improve margin, but there will be when the benchmark is always last year's product instead of the original launch item. Countless premium brand products slowly deteriorate beyond recognition because their quality is being reduced via tiny 'barely noticeable differences' which stack up to 'dramatic drop' over a longer period of time. And then it's too late to turn back. A better way to deal with sweating assets is revealed on page 65.

Last but not least, because this type of work is left to the juniors in the business who are still pretty clueless of the product, the category and the history, they will rely heavily on models (e.g. research) to make even the simplest decisions, rather than good ol' judgement. No market research can ever beat experience and a night's sleep for good decisions.

Sunny Smile Of **STRETCHING**

Innovating to redefine multiple marketing mix elements you normally play with. This can be about approaching new consumer targets in new occasions, through new channels. You're innovating to grow the category beyond its current boundaries. You're probably doing this because the space you started in is getting cramped and you are starting to feel pressure on pricing, with private label products going head to head with you on quality. It is a sign the category is evolving into one where stealing share will soon be the only way to grow.

I dare say that the greatest innovators distinguish themselves by repeatedly succeeding at stretching existing brands and businesses into new spaces, just beyond where they played before. They take the time to find that new insight[5], source that barrier-busting technology and craft the perfect product-packaging combination. They care about exciting a new group of consumers they haven't seen before.

It's also a type of innovation that requires the most experienced team, combining creative & exploratory skills with commercial & operational savviness.

---

[5] *Not a fact, trend or snippet of data. Insight is uncovering a consumer motivation or frustration (why) with enough context (who/what/when/where) to generate new ideas. 'Nough said.*

Murky Mechanics Of <u>STRETCHING</u>

Pitfalls and bear clamps appear simply from human nature when you put different disciplines in the same room and ask them to cooperate. This is aggravated in Stretch for a number of reasons:

- Stretch is Opportunity-led rather than Calendar-led. The upside is that the opportunity is likely to be in an established market, which means it can be quantified. The downside is that you don't know up front what form it will have, so the importance & roles of internal functions won't crystallize for some time into the investigation.
- Functions need to work largely in parallel in the early stages, rather than the more sequential split of roles in incremental innovation.
- The leadership must be function-agnostic and empathetic to grasp the very different personality types and KPI's that drive decision making across the disciplines involved.
- The monetary risk that comes with the opportunity is often huge. More work needs to be done and big investments are likely for new manufacturing equipment. Leadership gets nervous and demands silly levels of detail for the value of a still hypothetical opportunity.

Clearly, it's a people thing. Stretch works well when you can get a group of people who know what they're doing to use their expertise differently.

Sunny Smile Of **GAME CHANGERS**

Game-changing, aka Breakthrough, is what pops up in most people's minds when they think of innovation. It's the aspirational activity of laying trails instead of following them. Fame awaits.

I suspect that this type of clean-slate innovation isn't Opportunity-led but Personality-led. When you're part of such initiatives, it certainly feels more like a movement than a project, following someone's vision of the future. It's why such projects are better ignited by a manifesto than a spec sheet. Clarify *why* you're innovating, breaking barriers, instead of *what* you're trying to do. More in the last chapter (p.113).

Looking for easy ways to define what your category game changer would be like? Two tips:

- Try the four TRIZ dimensions on page 23.
- Ask yourself: "what competitor's launch would keep me awake at night?" Then go develop that.

The major difference with both previous types is that game changers often require a new business model.

The reason start-ups can take on existing businesses is they have a product, then look for niche models & channels to monetize it where the big guys aren't in yet. Corporate entities work the other way around: they have established operations and look for ideas they can monetize through it efficiently.

Murky Mechanics Of <u>GAME CHANGERS</u>

Breakthrough is about re-writing the rules and creating a new market. As a consequence, any assumption on feasibility, value or risk will be largely guesswork and based on gut feel of a very small group of people. They believe in it. Great. The problem is there's no real way of knowing if they're right or wrong. History is littered with failures by people with *exactly* the same conviction and persistence as those who became success stories.

A cynical reality is that businesses that need game changers most, those who have Six-Sigma'ed their way to commoditization, will have no such visionary characters left in their ranks. You cannot process-optimize your route to breakthrough success.

But when eventually does all come together and you consider the game changer itself, *version 2* is the one that will work and make some money. Version 1, the launch product everyone is banking on, will turn out merely a proof of concept. This is always the case, check the history books. Why? Because the newness is so dramatic. You cannot create something completely new *and* make it operationally efficient or reliable at the same time. That's not a problem, as long as it's acknowledged up front and the resources are there to work on v2 the moment v1 hits the ground – probably by a different team.

Then you walk away from your ailing cash cows.

Pulling this all together

Great innovators understand the intricacies of these three impact levels and the difference in mandate and mind-set they require to complete successfully. They understand when to ignite each type, as well as to what degree you can process-optimise them.

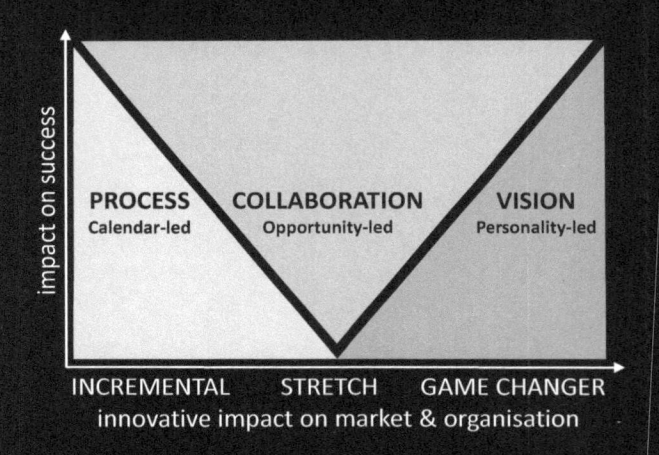

impact on success (y-axis)

PROCESS	COLLABORATION	VISION
Calendar-led	Opportunity-led	Personality-led

INCREMENTAL — STRETCH — GAME CHANGER
innovative impact on market & organisation

Looking at the impact levels above, one can see how 'Incremental' not only can, but *must* be caught in well-defined innovation processes as they guarantee long term ROI on innovation. But moving up to Stretching and Game Changing, the balance tilts to entrepreneurial. The processes that created the old markets have reached the end of their life-cycle and cannot deliver the breakthrough necessary to thrive in new markets of the future.

"Let's ask consumers what to choose!"
Someone who is...
A) A coward.
B) Ignorant to other success criteria.
C) Thinks consumers know how their business works.

Everything commodotizes, eventually. Everything.

There's a huge debate going on how to tune TV programming better to the interest of younger audiences. As if they still watch TV.

I suspect few people realise "wishful thinking" and "self-fulfilling prophecy" are inversely correlated, even mutually exclusive.

A change expert walks into bar
"This is all wrong"
"WTF?"
"You're analogue & you can't scale"
"FU & get out"
barman lives happily ever after

Be patient, time flies anyway.

Consumer research stating you lost on price
is likely to mean:
A) No real reason, you're just 'meh'.
B) They're fed up with the survey.

No matter how old & stale, some ideas remain new & fresh to people. Like the concept of remaining seated until the plane's reached the stand.

Wisdom of Crowds?
I'd say in the current state of affairs in the world, the crowds are the last ones I'd take advice from.

> *New movie pitch*
> **Evil super-villain invents unlimited eco-friendly energy source and then PATENTS it.**
> **"A license will be 100 $Bn, Mr Bond."**

A: "What did the moderator say to the plumber in the focus group?"
B: "You must be a lead user!"

Are you buying volume forecasting MR? SUCKER. Anyone who actually knows future revenue would be dealing on Wall St, not selling you MR.

Misunderstanding:
"Bankruptcy is OK as a start-up, investors value the experience". No, they prefer businesses run well over bankrupt ones."Oh you wanted a BIG idea?!"
Quickly hides pig under desk

Your strategy might be all about market penetration & building core, but don't forget at times your retail and distribution buyers just want something new.

The best moment to start working on that amazing innovation is about a year ago.
Same for writing that book.

> **Homeopathy was invented when an American coffee company accidentally made their brew too strong.**

[1st Place Attitude] - [2nd Place Attitude] = [Ego]

If you've delegated direct client contact to a talking computer, you're showing your vision for innovation is efficiency, not service levels.

Hey SME leadership. When considering a country to expand to, ask yourself if you'd like to travel there every month before doing business cases.

Only people who regularly speak with their customers will be worried about losing them.
Come down from your tower.

When perfectionists consider their jobs done; in reality it's either too soon or too late.

(things that give me energy) / (things that drain my energy) = midlife crisis tipping point.

Hey marketer, follow the money. Parents with most cash to spend are those at the age their kids have left the house. Get with the times.

Is your breakthrough innovation really v2.0?
Or just v1.1? What barrier is it really breaking?

Anyone can plot implications. Only few oversee implications of implications and it's usually the team at the executional end of the strategy.

In hindsight, every innovation turns out to be just another halfway-point between what was before and what came after. Even game changers.

Hey Food & Beverage Innovators - the world has reached 'Peak Calorie'. Focus on getting people to eat and drink differently, not more.

In market dev context, many charlatans implies unevolved, infancy market. Maturing, commodotizing markets shake out the fraudsters.

At the table, or on the menu? Those are your options in a competitive market.

Perfectionism in implementing v1 works only if you've already started work on v2 in the background. No one-hit wonders.

[The business equivalent of raising your chances of success is to flip a bigger coin.]

I suspect Stevia was tested only as a written concept.

Entrepreneurial: accepts ambiguity in present, yearns solid future goal. Operational: yearns solidity in present, accepts future ambiguity.

2nd grumpy innovator

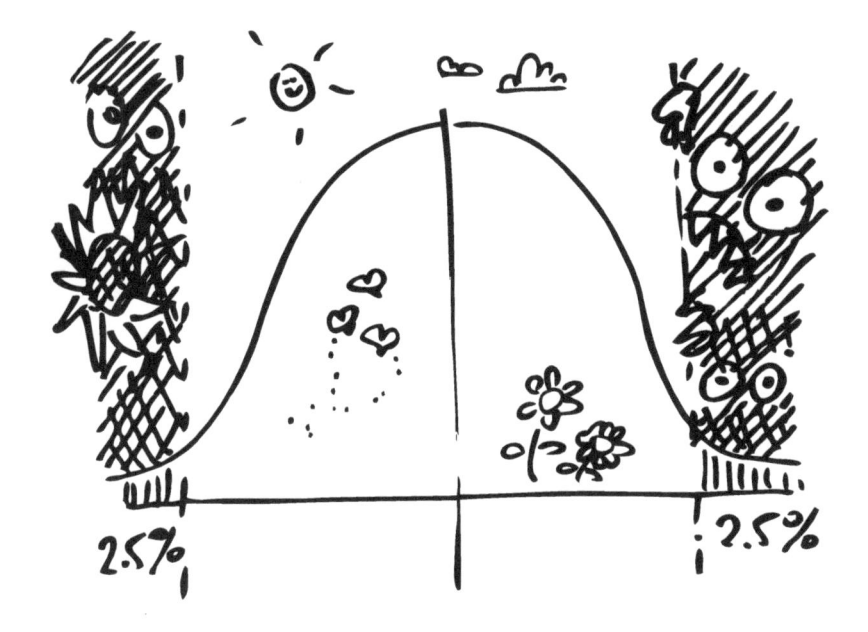

RISK IS THE SCARY STUFF *OUTSIDE* OF THE CONFIDENCE INTERVALS

Don't struggle downhill, that's just a silly waste of energy.

Hey Start-up, burning someone else's cash is not a business model. Sorry.

"Brave Visionary" and "Pig-headed Fool" are often only one feasibility proof-point apart.

"Dig a hole in the ground and run a train through? But the ground is for planting turnips"
Initial response to 1863 inventor of the metro.

Everyone, without exception, is risk averse. We just differ in the size of the risk we're averse to. Vive la différence.

The day you start believing your own spin, accidents will happen. Stay away from heavy machinery and don't drive a business until you sober up.

Have you noticed how founders of start-ups love calling themselves "CEO"? And never "Secretary General"? Except maybe in France.

Hey VC. If your model is hoping to sell hyped share to the next sucker, then you're building a Ponzi scheme, not a business model.

Here's a suggestion for a better quant validation score levels; "Failure" - "Risky" - "Ready" - "Outstanding" - "You Cheated The Model".

What doesn't kill you, probably almost kills you, therefore makes you weaker, more neurotic and paranoid for anything like it the future.

Note that when celebrating top-2 box scores, chest bumps are inappropriate. Save those for not being de-listed in year 2 after launch.

Fail Faster? Can we please agree Fail Less instead?

Launch in 9 months? Not if you can't register a new vendor in less than 3. Or send an email through your Citrix firewall in under 5 minutes.

IF CAR DASHBOARDS WERE DESIGNED THE SAME WAY AS CORPORATE DASHBOARDS.

Hey Start-up, remember you're building a business, not a product. That nuance will largely determine your level of success.

[Even if you are not the category leader, there's no harm in acting like one.]

'Conclusions' are drawn from research, they live within its scope. 'Insights' are triggered by research, but are agnostic to its scope.

[Quant concept screening should include a 'pisses off competition' metric.]

Invisible & intangible system tech (internet) is more fertile BS ground for quacks than visible & tangible tech (engines, bridges).

Businesses innovate & grow their value themselves. Raw materials' value only fluctuates by scarcity & hype from others.

The only trend watchers you should trust are the self-made billionaire ones. And they probably won't tell you anything.

"Turn around, look back and see the best is behind you" < see what I did there?

$1Bn VC opportunity on offer: 3D printed drones that Snapchat pictures of taxis. You're welcome.

Categories where pricing's dependent on fads/whims will always be outrun by industrial productivity. You can't innovate gold.

With that big decision coming up, you'd probably do better with less data and more sleep.

Snorkels, gas masks, trumpets and referee whistles. Products that are all in dire need of real breaththrough innovation. That's a pun.

Ask not: "how much pain will it take before something changes?"
Ask: "how much good will create the momentum for change?"

[The scarcest resource in innovation isn't Money, but Time.]

Hey VP R&D, Technical capability you want to excel at: develop and patent like there's no tomorrow. Because there is.

Riddle: "Who pays for innovation?"

ANSWER: Innovation pays for the innovation.

If your category is segmented, consider UN-segmenting it for a change. You'll be surprised.

Coupons - vision, strategy or tactic? Discuss.

Intermezzo: Sh*t analogies in business.

Childish banter – yes, definitely. But in today's cross-cultural corporate teams, I've found fecal analogies* to be a great universal language for expressing and defusing Murky situations.

When seeing poor crisis management:
Don't deal with shit by stamping on it.

When you are dressing up a bad idea to nudge it past a critical decision maker:
You can't polish a turd. But you *can* roll it in glitter.

When you want to cut through group paralysis or blame storming over a failed process:
Passing this shit around just gets everyone's hands dirty. Deal with it now FFS.

When you feel someone is asking too many unhelpful questions about what is an acute problem:
If it's brown and sticky, it's probably not ice cream.

When you know you're about to be presented a dud: **I don't need to see shit in order to smell it coming.**

When someone is wasting time classifying a whole range of bad options, to find the least bad one:
Here's a funny thing about bird shit: you know what that shiny little black speck is, sitting in the middle of all that white shit? That speck is *also* shit.

Sources unknown, but brilliant minds no doubt.

> **Breakthrough is about resolving category barriers, not your own manufacturing limitations.**

Big Data #1: "Measure to Control" - Yeah right. I've been measuring my penis for years and still can't control it.

Big Data #2: "You can't manage what you can't measure" - Which is misunderstood as that you should manage everything you can measure.

Big Data #3: "Live feed for decision making" - Your business will be in constant panic, unable to distinguish noise from signal.

Hotel Reception: where SUPPLY ("Let me express my amazing warm hospitality with a friendly chat") and DEMAND ("Just give me my room key now please") lie furthest apart.

Disruptive innovation pisses off the market leader. So if you're the market leader and you're asking for disruption, know what you ask for.

"New formula!" and "New recipe!"
The optimist's way of keeping a smile while value engineering.

Hey start-up, the VC is not gambling with his money, he's gambling with you. Just so you know.

"Now with extra [core benefit]"
The easiest and most overlooked way to create new propositions for your pipeline.

If you're innovating to grow revenue, don't forget improving distribution for some quick wins.

"MY EYES! THE PAIN! AAAARGH!"
First human pushing through category barriers to pursue the idea of chopping onions for dinner.

Wisdom of Crowds, or Wisdom of Bookmakers?
I know who I'd trust more with my money.

Did you know that hinged cell phones went extinct because of the discomfort for men with sideburns?

Yes, breakthrough innovation drives behaviour change. But if you're suggesting ADDING a step in the ritual, it ain't gonna happen.

Has crowd funding ever led to a sustainable new business? Or is it really just all one-off product launches? A bit like the movie industry I guess.

Figures should be taken figuratively. Not literally. Hence their name, 'figures'.

Cutting costs is not a strategy - it is a necessity after failed strategy.

WOULD YOU LIKE IT MORE
IF IT WERE 3D PRINTED?

PhD's that involve developing tools/products for fast moving consumer markets ... better speed up because 4 years lead time is too long.

Mass market essentials that have evolved to niche luxuries; vinyl, horses, fishing, V8 engines, C64 OS and pinball machines.

Hey, marketing manager. Had Twitter done what you have done in the past five years, these aphorisms would now be 350 characters, in colour.

To everyone stating that innovation is a linear & logical process - which ancient Olympic activity did Trampolining evolve from? See? See?

[**Hey start-up, it's not the quality of your idea that counts, but your ability to generate a cash flow.**]

Hey UX designer, consider your interface not an access, but a barrier between users and the product benefits. Your design will improve.

When your category/market is still immature, your innovation tactics should about differentiating from the quacks, clowns and frauds.

On transferring breakthrough innovation between categories; it's time that supermarket self-scanning migrates to airport security scanning.

A consumer panel recruiter walks into a bar. Everyone noticing the clipboard in time quickly leaves.

When you're clutching at straws at the fuzzy front end of innovation, it's better to clutch at fewer, stronger straws than more, weaker ones.

Reverse engineering stories around products that created a Paradigm Shift is also known as Marketing Bullshift.

> **If you don't grow the pond, you will deplete the pond, eventually.**

Audits won't increase your innovation capability, but accelerate the opposite by chasing away innovative colleagues.

On innovation timelines
1 "Yonk" equals
5 "Dog years" equals time for
10 "Cows to come home"?

The fact not all shit-hot innovations from the US work in Europe or vice versa boils down to the Fahrenheit-Celsius conversion.

If you choose to create an innovation team merely to please the investors, be aware your successor may end up less pleased. So who cares?

> **"Oh no, you're doing it all wrong!"**
> *All strategy experts, upon seeing their theories brought to practice.*

Whatever you think is 50-50 is probably 80-20. And your 80-20 is probably 99-1.

> **Break the category rules before they break you.**

Type P-A-R-A-D-I-G-M then press SHIFT. Notice how nothing happens? I thought the same. Overrated.

When you set off to improve your consumer's shopping experience, don't forget to involve the retailer. What's in it for them?

A failed innovation isn't an innovation, just a failure. Which every innovation is, until it's succeeded.

Maybe letting go of your old cash cows is easier if you give them a full Viking funeral?

Stop whining about category intrinsic barriers. They're true for your competition as much as yourself. It's up to you to break them.

Category generic attributes are not a smart bet to build your proposition around. They're not ownable, that's why they're called generic.

Rather than ranking benefits, ask which benefits your target is willing to sacrifice for the one that really matters.

When marketers forget which part of their brand's heritage was true and which was spin, press 'record' and enjoy the show.

The more desperate you are for new ideas, the more likely you are to follow the wrong ones when they finally appear.

The difference between short term and long term innovation is improving a product versus improving a proposition. That's all.

"Wait, I really need to put more thought into this."
Engineer who really needs to make a prototype.

2nd grumpy innovator

Build The Brand & Own The Copy

CAN'T WE JUST BUY THIS FROM THE SUPERMARKET ACROSS THE ROAD AND REPACKAGE IT AS OUR OWN?

Build The Brand & Own The Copy

Innovation in fast moving consumer goods & services – it's a tough world where the winners take all, right? Not necessarily.

Let's start by looking at the world of innovation through the eyes of branded goods companies. Looking inward, innovation is a difficult endeavour. It's all about juggling creative effort, consumer needs and technical capabilities; then convincing the channel owners you're the right partner to launch your grand ideas. You're on a knife's edge, finding the right balance between innovative leaps and operational reality, creating something new but not too new. Looking outward, it's a bloody war. Even if you successfully manage to outrun competition, your channel partners soon turn their back on you and start knocking off copies of the product you worked so hard to dream up and scrape a profit from.

Looking at the world of innovation through the eyes of a private label brand, life's not much easier. You manage a bazillion different categories under one and the same name, continuously looking for ways of improving quality and building the trustworthy reputation that will drive traffic through your stores' aisles. And just when you get that mix right, shoppers desert you for the discounters.

You might think: "It's all so unfair, with so many losers. And what a waste of energy."

Note that this is the space of Incremental and Stretch innovation, the supposedly 'easier' end of the spectrum.

An ugly truth driving both scenarios is that everything commoditizes. Nothing new remains new for very long and it proves that successful innovation is one that appears mundane in no-time, no matter how breakthrough it first seemed. Whether you like it or not, your unique advantage will be copied and move down the ranks of specialness – sooner rather than later.

Another ugly truth is that only innovation can pay for innovation. Whatever new thing you do, it'll need to pay for itself and earn back the CapEx you invested to get it made. You need to show an ROI quick or it'll simply not be worth the risk. You are always in a hurry. When the Branded and Private Label perspectives see each other as adversarial, that ROI timeline looks roughly as follows:

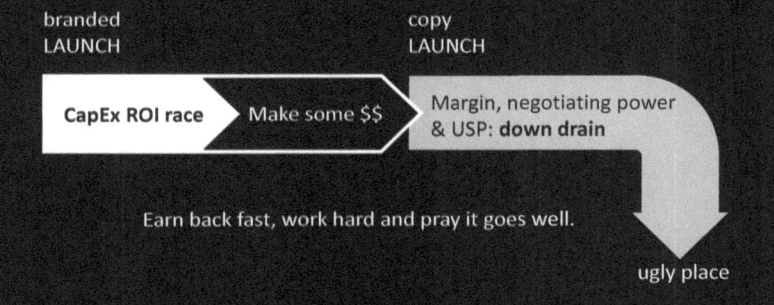

branded
LAUNCH

copy
LAUNCH

CapEx ROI race — Make some $$ — Margin, negotiating power & USP: **down drain**

Earn back fast, work hard and pray it goes well.

ugly place

The Branded team launches a new product, then works like crazy to earn back the investment and hopefully has enough time left for making a bit of money before a Private Label copy is put on shelf right next to it. The only apparent solution is to run even harder on making that ROI happen faster.

Given it is virtually impossible to create products that cannot be copied, in particular in fast moving consumer goods & services, this scenario is painful. Not because of its unfairness but because of its short-sightedness. It's equal to ignoring, even running away from the inevitable.

What's more, the only possible next step for the branded team is to lower their price, which spirals into a fight that cannot be won. Red oceans are great for the underdog, not for the top predator.

The key to unlocking this conflict is understanding both parties' common ground: they both need assets to create their goods. The CapEx required to create truly innovative products is high, and in the scenario above is in fact spent twice; once for the original and then again for the copy. Not only are Branded and Private Label teams destroying each other's cash flow in price combat, they both start that war in debt. What a waste of resources, effectively shrinking the category value.

Dear Branded goods team: the answer is ever so simple. Own the copy. When you invest heavily in new assets to create new branded products, ensure you also own the capacity needed to create the copies that will eventually be made. Instead of hoping the PL knock-off will never come, agree with the retailers you'll create their copies after a grace period. It makes your future easier to plan and spreads your ROI over a much longer period. What's more, you can make agreements with multiple retailers and if there's one thing that drives down cost, it's *volume*.

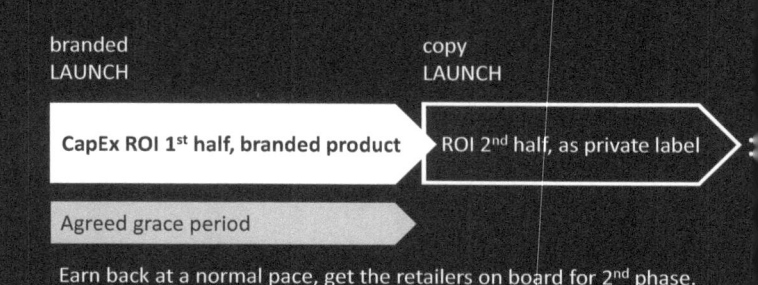

branded LAUNCH   copy LAUNCH

CapEx ROI 1st half, branded product → ROI 2nd half, as private label →

Agreed grace period

Earn back at a normal pace, get the retailers on board for 2nd phase.

Dear Private Label team: accept that grace period and save

yourself some money and arm twisting to get a high quality product on shelf.

What's the catch? There is none, other than that branded teams need to address their innovation cycles differently.

impact on market ↑

Game Changing innovation is out of scope for now.

1 **Stretch** innovation, create new product, service or packaging platforms, requiring big CapEx. Launch as BRANDED goods, develop market while agreeing phase 2 with Private Labels.

2

Incremental innovation, rapid cycles of improvement for branded product using same assets, launch Private Label copy one iteration behind. Start work on next Stretch platform for future.

→ **time passes & market evolves**

If you know you're giving away the crown jewels, you need to have the next generation lined up and ready to go. In essence, you work on two innovation pipelines at the same time.

1. Long cycle Stretch innovation, creating the new standards for your branded product that require big CapEx investment. This is *literally* the next generation platform, the new manufacturing line that secures future relevance of your branded product.

2. Short cycle Incremental innovation, strengthening your branded product with small iterations. The moment the Private Label copy goes live, the branded product you're running on the same line should start receiving small value-adds. Sweat the asset so you're continuously

keeping your branded goods one step ahead and worth their premium pricing.

And then the story starts all over – but with more winners this time. You can even imagine a 3rd step, after a few years when the PL comes on board to the new platform, you milk the old assets for the new table guests: the Discounters.

> ```
> >>> SIDE STEP ON SWEATING ASSETS
> ```
>
> In the typical operational view on Sweating assets, the goal is to optimize production and cut cost out of the product without any (perceivable) change for the consumer. Which in practice *always* leads to iterative loss of product experience & quality.
>
> A more productive and rewarding approach is to commission a manufacturing team to "show how this kit might create new features that add value for our customer without incremental cost". Or push it even further, "Where would you love to add 5% cost in this product?".
> The response will initially shock and paralyze, as it'll never have been asked before. Followed by a suggestion to spend it on quality control, which isn't the point either. But eventually a creative engineering team will shift from a cost-saving attitude to the more rewarding value-adding mentality.
>
> The culture you grow this way bridges a classic consumer-tech divide in many businesses, in two simple ways;
>
> - Technical teams become skilled at translating features into benefits and vice versa, all the way through to manufacturing assets.
>
> - There is less intention to commission assets that are 'singular' execution optimized, and instead choose for embedding flexibility for future product variations.
>
> Sweating assets is often mistaken for a short term solution to resolve production cost issues.
>
> **WRONG:** MOST EFFICIENCY GAINS LEAK AWAY AS ASSET UNDERUTILISATION, NOT MARGIN.

> ```
> If you make products with 20% less asset use, but
> have nothing to fill that spare capacity with,
> you're not being very truthful to the goal, right?
>
> On the other hand, a manufacturing team with a
> value-add mindset can turn any production facility
> into a sustainable, progressive, incremental
> innovation power house, funding future success and
> keeping the pressure on the business to move
> forward.
> ```
>
> <<< END OF SIDE STEP

A brave leadership eventually shifts incremental innovation responsibility entirely to operational teams, in particular circumstances where portfolio management is so heavily restricted by manufacturing guardrails, it is *asset* management that defines its success. Sales and Manufacturing are then in charge of the short term pipeline of products, connecting any shifting customer & consumer demands directly to manufacturing & delivery improvements[6]. Putting the short term responsibility for change amongst those who actually implement it also frees R&D and Marketing functions up to look at future opportunities that will drive the next platform-level technology. Win-Win.

That said, it is a brave stance in a mass market industry where MBA & Marketing skewed disciplines seem to pull most of the innovation strings. Plenty focus on strategy yet little interest in how their products are actually made. This needs to change[7].

[Insert Grumpy groan here, then have a coffee]

---

[6] *Ironically, this is how things are run in practice in many global companies already, especially those believing their global brand teams are in charge of innovation. They're not (our little secret).*

[7] *And it slowly is... SWEAT® & 'voice of technology' are playing an ever bigger part in the innovation projects we run with our clients.*

Maybe Homeopathic should rebrand itself as Nanoconcentrated or Hyperhydrated?

Then, just as you phase out production of the old stuff to launch your shiny new product, some client places a huge order for the old crap.

Hey Airline. When boarding a shuttle-bus to the plane, I'd rather forgo my frequent flyer rights and board LAST, thanks.

The first successful focus groups were run 2,000 years ago among 3x4 respondents (1 lapsed user) on a concept with 'faith' as only RTB.

"Looking for concepts with benefits"
Lonely marketer ad

The person who created your smartphone's autocorrect algorithm tested the concept in focus groups as "cellophane autocratic algae rhythm".

Think not: "How do I add a feature?"
Think instead: "How do I remove a step between consumer and end benefit?"

The "iconic" in "iconic packaging" is probably not what's stopping your consumers from abandoning you for better packaged competition.

Over 37%" or "Almost 40%" - framing.

Hey Recording Artist, if you want a truly global audience, get listed as teleconference holding music. Only problem is people will hate you.

Yo Momma's so fat she fills all quartiles.

Red oceans are full of opportunity (for the underdog, not for the top predator).

> **A Unique Selling Point for your product will be cancelled out by lots of Generic Disappointing Points.**

It's easier to de-risk a risky opportunity than to de-bland a bland one.

Hey marketer, most female consumers are NOT moms. And if they are they have only 1.4 kids who bug dad too. Get with the times.

Don't walk into a meeting with your boss 15 minutes late while holding a Starbucks coffee.

My other $1Bn idea for cheap airline travel: charge $10 for a barf bag. Probably $20 would work too.

Note: 'hybrid' is usually the temporary compromise between the old and whatever little bit of new that will eventually be the new normal.

The fairy tale of service innovation always ends with them living happily ever after-sales.

The business growth analogy of building a car while you're driving it is incomplete. You're also doing it with a blinking fuel gauge light.

> **"But status quo is also status!"**

In the canteen of life, we all have a gravy recipe to cover up for bad cooking.

Are you moving your portfolio up into premium or democratising it downwards?

If you bring 'lean' and 'innovation' under responsibility of the same team/person, guess what topic they'll spend all their time on.

Americans are not worried about their privacy in social media. Just look at their public toilet stalls, they have no concept of privacy.

"OMG I AM GOING TO SLIP AND DIE, NAKED"
What everyone thinks, stepping out of a hotel bathtub shower.

If you have an international user survey to run, set up a kiosk at Dubai airport T3. Everyone's here.

"Buy one, get one free? How kind of this brand's sales & marketing team!"
No shopper, ever. The retailer gets all the credit.

If you consider your personal opinion as representative for your target audience, you're classifying your thoughts as perfectly average.

> **Warm-up and flex your mirror neurons before engaging in consumer research.**

A super-power most marketers have is being able to jump to conclusions faster than a speeding bullet.

So you created a 3-year plan to move up from 5th place to 1st place? And what do you think number 4, 3 & 2 are doing in the meantime?

Somewhere, someone's making a living out of the exact opposite of what you do.

[Batman voice] The concept's benefit statement you wrote. It's not single minded.

I'm a bit disappointed to see this airport's six ePassport gates simply link through to a security dude with six screens.

Remember the Microsoft Office Assistant paper clip? I do. Regularly. Usually at night, chasing me in my dreams with unsolicited advice.

Cab drivers binary syntax for waiting times:
"10 minutes" < 30 minutes
"10-15 minutes" > 30 minutes

Descriptions you really don't want to hear/read about yourself: "Increasingly disturbing", "Harmless", "Pre-diabetic", "Loud" & "Too close".

Italic or Bold or Underline. OR please. Not AND.

LOW HANGING FRUIT IS PROBABLY STILL HANGING THERE FOR A REASON.

Remember the days when you could boost sales with a "Free Toy Inside" without being told off for killing your margin?

Most products and services are a means to an end, not an end in itself. Which means people prefer less of it. Not more.

[**Don't worry about a decision tree for the people buying your product. Worry about one for people NOT buying your product.**]

"Designed in [country]" beats
"Made in [country]" beats
"Shipped by [country]" beats
"Mined in [country]"

Stevia is the universe's way of telling me I should cut down on sweeteners.

I think there's an opportunity for soft drink suppliers to absorb some of the world's excess carbon dioxide: "Now with 100% natural CO_2".

[**As kids grow up, emergencies shift from physical to social.**]

Screening out the bad ideas doesn't mean the ones you're left with are any good. Ideas must be developed, not screened.

Developers of wearable technology seem to overlook that the world is not 100% populated by hypochondriacs. Any non-health apps out yet?

Hey digital revolution, you cannot eat internet.

"TOO MUCH HAIR" & "TOO MUCH SKIN"
SOME LINKEDIN PROFILE PHOTOS

"Boolean Communication Gap"
When you say AND AND AND your audience hears OR OR OR. And vice versa.

An example of a message that packs both good and bad news into one: "Beards and tattoos are going out of fashion".

> [great product] + [shit packaging]
> = [untapped potential]
> **BUT**
> [shit product] + [great packaging]
> = [pending trouble]

BoM rot. When value engineering transcends into removing value-add components.

NPD: "Now does [new thing]"
EPD: "Now does [old thing] better"

"Because it's [MyBrandName]" is a very poor RTB and an even worse benefit.

You can recognize anyone who grew up with MsDOS by their discomfort with spaces in file names. And they refer to directories, not folders.

Just paid $6.90 for a small Starbucks cappuccino at GVA airport and learned what price elasticity physically feels like.

"Operational innovation success" anagrams to "super-conventional association".
Remember, you read it here first.

Hey retailer, so your business model is to run at a loss all year through to November and then correct everything in December? Really?

"Stevia", not as sweet as it sounds.
"Steve" would be more appropriate.

> **Riddle:**
>
> | | | | |
> |---|---|---|---|
> | *Miromesnil* | *Lourmel* | *Daumesnil* | *Buzenval* |
> | *Solferino* | *Duroc* | *Tolbiac* | *Hoche* |
> | *Dupleix* | *Vavin* | *Botzaris* | *Raspail* |
> | *Corentin* | *Simplon* | *Alésia* | |
>
> **Names for OTC & R$_x$ drugs or Paris metro stations?**
>
> ANSWER: Paris metro stations

Private Label teams talk about Discounters just like Brand teams talked about PL teams 10 years ago ("they're lower quality"). There's a storm coming.

Don't get angry with Operations when they scrap your idea being for 'too expensive' if you didn't check their capabilities before you started.

[**Don't take credit for a 1% upward movement of a quarterly sales figure unless you're OK taking blame for a 1% downward one.**]

I suspect most people complaining about lack of good ideas simply don't know what a good idea looks like.

"NO I'm NOT too drunk to worrrk!" - the civil engineer who planned the roads to/from Leeds-Bradford Airport.

Probably the most anticipated automotive innovation for Mercedes owners is a feature that stops them being hailed as taxis.

Middle management is all about managing senior management.

Hey Market Researcher, how sure are you that your heavy users aren't just big boned?

Imagine your kitchen trash can asking "Are you sure you want to delete this?" every time you toss something in.

> **That colleague you think is a wonk thinks you are a fluff fairy.**

"We need more chrome & wood!", said automotive marketing manager who needs a lot less plastic.

"Me too!!"
Most product launches

Viagra teams in Pfizer's corporate offices must have real issues getting their emails past spam filters.

World Procrastination Day, postponed again. :-(

Failure post-mortems: the vain assumption that although success factors eluded you, those for analysing failure are within your grasp.

The difference between a consumer 'need' and 'want' is expressed in the level of guilt felt in between consumptions.

1.4Bn cups of coffee are poured around the globe every day. That means there are at least 5.6Bn people with some explaining to do.

Ignorant Innovation Pundit Fallacy: mistaking 'Can Imagine' for 'Can Do'. Creating ideas is easy, creating business streams isn't.

> **Inspiration didn't fail you.
> You failed Inspiration.**

The middle word in "insight" is "sigh".

Your competition will thank you for promoting category benefits.

You say "neether", I say "naither".
You say "tomaato", I say "tomahto".
You say "top-2 box PI%", I say "small test market".

Ask any consumer for an opinion and they'll give you one. Not because they have one, but because you asked for one.

Youkea or Ikea?

"This product could do with a lot less salt", said the food brand manager tasting a prototype that could do with a lot more real ingredients.

The expression "back to the drawing board" only briefly evolved into "back to SolidWorks" and has now settled as "back to Outlook"?

> **Amazing how market researchers look for that one thing in humans that all humans dread being seen as: average.**

If packaging requires using your teeth to open, I think you can safely say it's a design failure. In particular for cleaning products.

The difference between "nosy" and "curious" is about 25 cm, or 30 seconds, or 10 dB or 1 question too many.

When space is tight, the sequence of your actions becomes important. Development budgets, car parks, political coalitions & holiday packing.

Engineering Algorithm:
LOOP(3;($PromisedDate+99);3DCAD($Ideas);BUILD($Protot ype);BREAK($Prototype))+Flow($Tears)+FILE($Report)+HOME(5PM;END)

Lost in translation: "less trash" and "environmentally friendly" mean totally different things.

And then you realize you can blame EVERYTHING on the design team. Pfffew!

It's significantly more difficult to bullshit in Prototypes than it is in PowerPoints.

If you are hiring a lot of "Customer Retention Managers", then you are by definition hiring the wrong people, at the wrong end.

What is the complementary colour of brown?

"Yes this meeting room is hot. We're having a Bikram briefing session."

Hey global brand team, wondering how to make abstract strategy more tangible? Get someone with a local market P&L responsibility involved.

Great prank to mess up your Marketing colleague's concept scores: add "with free coupons" to the worst concept's benefit statement.

People dislike being average. They prefer being dynamic and exciting, aka a moving average.

"Whatever rattles is probably close to breaking." *Engineers talking about relationships.*

2nd grumpy innovator

Tail Wag Dog

NO, IT'S ACTUALLY EVEN WORSE THAN LAST YEAR'S PRODUCT. BUT AT LEAST THIS ONE IS IN LINE WITH OUR STRATEGY.

Tail Wag Dog

This chapter is about methodology[8], what happens when processes & tools mix with human nature.

Let me get this out of way: *I'm not against process*. In fact, I absolutely *love* smart methodologies and I get physically aggressive when people deviate from paths I know will lead them to good solutions. I'm a sucker for frameworks, 2x2's and I spent half my career marvelling at near-magical manufacturing logistics that bring thousands of parts to the right place at the right time in the right sequence.
It freaks me out when creative gurus approach challenges without structure "and let it come".

The expression 'tail wag dog' refers to a small part controlling the whole, be it in size, importance, attention or action. Consider it through the lens of innovation, creating new things:

```
"The result will be remembered long after
    the process has been forgotten."
```

There's a clear hierarchy expressed up there. The process supports creating a result. A better result via simpler/less process is always preferable over the other way around. In that sense *any* process is a compromise, because plucking a good result instantly from thin air would be an ideal situation[9].

---

[8] *Syntax note: "Methodology" is the term I use to rake together all tools, processes, frameworks, etc that support delivering results.*

[9] *Many business functions are a compromise for direct access to whatever they deliver. Would you still use consumer panels as a compromise to research your market if you could also have direct access to all of them via the internet or so? What, you CAN?!?*

Process Excellence's main purpose ~~is~~ *should* be to maintain or improve the value-add & quality of an outcome, whilst making the process itself obsolete.

Yet in many organisations, functions, teams – even inside people's heads – "process" and "result" become mixed up and draw attention away from what matters. Fulfilling the process becomes a goal in itself, disconnected from the outcome it is designed to deliver.

sexiness of tool ↑	OMG I want to do this all day	NIRVANA
	Sh*t	Chore to delegate

effectiveness of tool →

If you're wondering if this is the case for you or your team, check your gut response to this 2x2 chart for Methodology Qualification[10]. If you are attracted mainly to the X-axis, you are a result-focused person and you are probably lying. You are much more likely to rank your tools & methodologies along the Y-axis, like the tool-focused person we all are.

Humans love tools. Even before we properly stood upright, we were banging rocks together to create utensils that eased our lives. Our resourcefulness is expressed by our tools. Today's (innovation) equivalents exist across

---

[10] *inspired by Darrell Mann's Steak-vs-Sizzle analysis*

corporate functions and different abstraction levels. Tools, processes, hierarchies, stage gates, the ownership of which is often clustered in cost centres and staff functions.

So why are we such suckers for tools & process? Let's look at a couple of intriguing dimensions.

Personal Security

Tools & processes put a safe distance between yourself and the end result. More cynically: it puts distance between yourself and the consequences of your decisions. You can even say the process made the decision for you.

Also, you can blame a tool or process in infinitely more than you can blame an end result. Processes can be blamed for wasting your time, creating poor outputs, being imprecise, improperly validated, too wide or too narrow. But an end result can be connected directly to your decisions and actions.

Perception Of Control And Being In Charge

Our OCD tendency for control via tools is worsened further by technical advances enabling us to measure everything around us, right from our tablets. The fact you can measure it doesn't mean you can control it, nor that the information is supporting to better end result.

The perception of control is quite perverse; in particular in innovation where even at the most operational end of the spectrum (Incremental innovation) it is still a creative effort. One can for example be fooled that a validation framework to *judge* ideas is also suitable to *create* them. Creators use different thinking styles and frameworks from reviewers – and both are valid. The ugly part is that in Western corporate hierarchies, reviewers often sit higher up the food chain than the creators. It's led to the amazing reality that lower ranks are praised for creating ideas and the higher ranks for not stopping them. As if they're competing.

Perception Of Thoroughness

A process-heavy initiative will feel like a thorough one, with lower risk. Add in acronyms like PDCA, FMEA, RACI or DMAIC and we'll all expect things to be OK, in fact we'll even ignore things that are not presented to us through our processes and tools. Understandable for Incremental innovation when the calendar is on your heels. Yet quite counter-productive behaviour if you are engaging in Stretch or Game Changing innovation, where the opportunities must by definition come from places you haven't before looked, measured or analysed.

Collecting huge piles of data also raises the chances of finding large swathes of *conflicting* data, which confuses more than it enlightens. What were previously singular outliers which could inspire or be ignored, now become a statistical nuisance that need to be explained *within* the model.

Bad Before Good Feels Good

Humans are primarily fear driven creatures, as a creative consequence we're much better at finding problems than we are finding solutions. We enjoy it more too. When presented with a new idea, we revel in pinpointing all its flaws and then walk away into the sunset, feeling like we actually helped[11].

As a consequence, many processes and decision making structures are designed around evading wrong paths, rather than seeking the right ones.

Two examples to make that less abstract:

- Reviews after (innovation/launch) failure, aka post-mortems. It is quite amusing considering that teams who didn't grasp the requirements to succeed will confidently go about identifying why it all would have failed. But what makes the activity even more counter-productive is that it always ends with an *even stricter* set of criteria for launch, making success *ever more unlikely* to happen. Think about this one, it's a gem.

- Screening rather than developing ideas. Too many innovation funnels are purely selective, losing potential winners along the way because the whole package didn't meet expectations, rather than iteratively expanding the parts that do work over time. Where screening might work for Incremental, in Stretch and Game Changing you'll cull too soon and for the wrong reasons.

---

[11] *No, this isn't helpful <u>at all</u>.*

You Can Manipulate Methodology

Ending this journey downward at cynical depths before crawling back up; Humans simply love cheating the system. 'Beating it' as they will say themselves. Maybe not true for everyone, but definitely for the type of person working in a competitive marketing/R&D/operations leadership function in innovation. Processes are connected to KPI's and they are *so* much easier to manipulate than end results. The frightening thing is it happens with positive intent. All of the previous paragraphs show how hiding, hogging, hoarding, hitting and halting behaviours can be interpreted as being productive and serving the cause. Re-writing an identical concept 10x in order to get it past a hurdle defined by a quantitative test populated by a huge but non-representative sample of survey-loving people, ranking on measurable but irrelevant parameters? It happens all the time and with the best intent of following procedures.

GRUMPIEST POINT REACHED. FROM HERE ON WE GO UP.

Anyone with more than one product or service launch on their name will admit "Innovation Management' is a bit of an oxymoron. If anything, the innovation manages *you* and you just try to hang onto it and pass the finishing line in one piece and roughly in the form you had in mind at the beginning. It is a game of compromise, persuasion and most of all – the one thing that clogs all stage gates and processes – navigating ***ambiguity***.

Over the years, I've found that the people most skilled at cheating systems put in place to manage innovation processes are *not* the evil ones driven by personal reward.

Instead, it is a special group that (at Happen Group) we refer to as **Innovation Rebels**.

For them, a Stage Gate is merely an obstacle course they know is part of the job.

The final chapter of this book is about them – hopefully you'll recognize a lot of yourself in it.

Free tips on next page!

Tail Wag Dog: Murky Process Focused

Looking across the spectrum of innovation, a few signs[12] of over-reliance on models and disconnection from the real world that drives successful outcomes.

	Incremental	Stretch	Game Changer
Voice of Mrkt Research	Use 5yr old Segmentation	Single piece of research at start	Ask consumers what they want
Voice of Technology	Change product formats	Ignore off-the-shelf solutions	Test only internally
Voice of Marketing	Create new brand	Launch globally all at once	Rotate to new job <12 months
Voice of Design	Redesign pack AND product	Ignore category archetypes	Use old pack design
Voice of Manufacturing	Ignore Sales team requests	Go straight to hard tooling	Order high-volume kit
Voice of Business	Put accountant in charge	No market support	Drive for Margin Improvement
Voice of Distribution	Change outer dimensions	Launch in wrong aisle	Default to existing channel
Voice of Supply Chain	Remove value instead of cost	Exclude existing suppliers	Run a 6σ optimisation
Voice of Boardroom	Assume this grows market	Assume this comes cheap	Overpromise @ City / Wall St

---

[12] Disclaimer: this list is not complete, obviously.

Dog Wag Tail: Sunny Result Focused

Attitudes and frameworks that drive successful outcomes in innovation, keeping a solid footing in the real world[13].

	Incremental	Stretch	Game Changer
Voice of Consumer	Validation with Lead Users	Competing categories	Validate in real test market
Voice of Technology	Recipe changes with new claims	Trial prototypes with Lead Users	Be paranoid & patent
Voice of Marketing	Steal market share	Find benefits to tweak habits	New UX & habits
Voice of Design	No heroics on product or pack	Go for big shelf presence	Be a hero
Voice of Manufacturing	Sweat Assets	Co-supply new components	Run 1st year on pilot lines
Voice of Business	Clear KPI's	Involve lead customers	Consider Skunk works option
Voice of Distribution	Keep logistic parameters	Choose aisle with customers	Road test in new channels
Voice of Supply Chain	Co-develop with suppliers	Work directly with R&D	Up/Re-skill the team
Voice of Boardroom	Provide realistic resource	Don't get in the way	Have faith in Rebel team

---

[13] Disclaimer: this list is not complete, obviously.

"Statistical confidence" anagrams to "facilitates disconnect". Remember, you read it here first.

> **Whatever the data says, it's still *your* decision.**

Dear inventors,
Big corporations are good at buying raw ingredients, people and other businesses. Not good at buying your ideas; they don't have a department for that.

So you had an amazing new product that consumers loved, but it failed and you say the market wasn't ready? Barriers are mostly INTERNAL.

'Consumer-centricity' methods are like harassing your friends for 'What do you want for your birthday?!?'. Don't ask, instead observe and surprise.

Knock knock!
"Who's there?"
"Would you like to fill in a survey?"
"Yes plz!"
Optimizes ideas for niche of nice people, who enjoy answering surveys

eCommerce suggestion engines don't offer you something new, but more of the same. You'll turn into a cliché of yourself.

Knock knock!
"Who's there?"
"Would you like to fill in a survey?"
"Hell no, go away."
Cleans data & corrects sample size to still appear relevant

Screw your 95% confidence. How about some "put your own money in this" confidence?

How long before a "temporary solution" no longer counts as such?

"Our insights are so good we call them WINsights. Get it?" - Market research salesperson about to be shown the door.

"That's not the kind of sample I had in mind"
Hands back cup to market researcher

"I. NEED. MOAR. DATAARGH"
Analyst drowning in data.

"Do as I see, not as I do."
Trend watcher raising children.

Really, are recorded customer service centre calls EVER used for training purposes? I'd prefer just training you directly.

I'M PRETTY SURE OUR PLANNING IS NOW UP TO DATE WITH WHAT REALLY HAPPENED

I'm not sure that 'ticking boxes' really counts as a result.

> **Processes are great places to hide in, even better than hierarchies.**

"Good insight, meagre benefit and rubbish RTB scores", said the market researcher reporting how global religions fare in a quant concept screener.

Captains of Industry have managed to create an Industry of Captains.

I think the world could do well with a "War On Error" right now. Too much stupidity around us, no?

"Hey, that's a perfect solution! And look here, another one! And another one!" - No perfectionist, ever.

"I probably already know the answer to this, right?" - What too few researchers ask themselves before doing more research.

*** BREAKING MARKET RESEARCH NEWS ***
Most consumers don't know their motivations either, so don't worry if you get it wrong too.

> **Shit forecasts can be recognized by the optimistic upswing being predicted as "just around the corner".**

Intelligence is less expressed through your amazing planning skills, and more by your actions when reality kicks your plan out the window.

In today's age project failure because of 'lack of communication' cannot be blamed on the tools. Not since the invention of the phone.

Data isn't analysed but interpreted. Especially when there's lots of it. It's OK, just be aware of the difference. There's a human involved.

Spot the Millennial by their utter disrespect of file sizes. Emailing 6Mb pics of cats and 97Mb ppts with only 8 slides.

Are our lives really more busy & complicated nowadays, or are research companies just adding that question to surveys more often?

Process Excellence projects should always have as ultimate objective: "Make Money With This Process While Staying In Bed Sleeping".

Tomorrow I must buy Uber stock with the earnings from my Groupon and Zynga stock. Oh shit.

Dear regulator, are you making it easier to hire or more difficult to fire? Not the same.

Whenever I walk in the street and see an electric scooter, it's after I turn my head and think "holy s**t that thing could have killed me".

I just scanned and shredded all my tax paperwork from 1996 to 2014. Does anyone need a big bag of ultimate piñata filling?

If you base your decisions on reports, be aware you're basing them on filtered, processed information. That's not bad, just be aware it is.

[A 50% increase in innovation success rates doesn't mean much if it's reflecting a rise from 2% to 3% success.]

If you work in innovation, stating you're a perfectionist is a bad thing. You need iterations. Roughly right beats precisely wrong, always.

Setting stricter KPI's after a failure will in fact *decrease* the chance of future success.

Has there ever in human history been an instance that someone actually managed to sleep better with a travel neck-pillows?

Process guardian:
"Secure, prescriptive & fool-proof".
The process executive:
"FFS find me a loophole thru this sh*t".

The fact you just received a 200-page market research report is not an excuse for switching off your brain/gut and believe every word in it.

$\left[\begin{array}{l}\textbf{"My data is bigger than yours"}\\ \textit{\textbf{Market researcher with small penis}}\end{array}\right]$

The simpler your solution is, the more difficult it is to convince others of its value.
Audiences confuse complexity with rigor.

I'm not sure all this fitness tracking wearable technology is making humanity any fitter.

I wonder how many market research agencies use their own qual & quant methodologies to develop new propositions for their clients.

"I will make big decisions on the likeliness that a paid respondent says they might promote our product to someone else, who then might follow that unsolicited advice and buy it, even though people can't even predict correctly what they will buy themselves when we ask them directly."
NPS in practice.

If you insist on doing innovation according to this long & tedious stage-gate process, plz show me the successes it brought you before.

[Consumer segmentation. Or what the rest of us call Stereotyping.]

The one thing I can guarantee Big Data will never predict, is the demise of Big Data.

Hey Product Designer, design is a means to an end, not an end in itself. If you believe otherwise, sign your work and sell it in a gallery.

I'm not staring at my phone, I'm checking the state of world affairs, OK?

Never forget that "market research" is a compromise for not being able to speak to all your consumers personally. A map, not reality.

Can someone explain me the logic behind Gatwick's Airport's Sky Bridge again? I forgot.

Complaining the taxi to the airport is more expensive than the flight itself? Take the bus to the airport next time.

In a 1,000 years BGY airport will be dug up by archaeologists and mistaken for a cologne factory.

BUT IF YOU *DID* GIVE A SHIT ABOUT THIS PRODUCT, WHAT WOULD YOU LIKE ABOUT IT?

However desirable it sounds, note that for whatever you track 'real time' it becomes VERY difficult to distinguish signal from noise.

Is there a process for being result-focused?

Put any quant market researcher in trouble by asking what type of people are willing to fill in 20 minute surveys. Not representative.

Quant agencies are insisting concepts are written ever shorter. Not for higher sales in market, but lower drop-out rates in surveys.

When you're lost, you prefer NO directions over knowingly WRONG directions. Yet in market research, the it seems absolutely fine.

"Who would like to join our committee to discuss ways of reducing non-value-add operational projects and processes?"

> **Has your Lean/6σ VP suggested ways to make his/her own team obsolete yet? I thought so.**

That fact it appears disorganised doesn't automatically mean it is inefficient or unproductive.

Somewhere, some person is claiming that Big Data predicted all of this, in hindsight.

Hey Strategist, tell me about all the massive innovation successes you've ignited by stacking Excel sheet data. One example will do, thanks.

"Let's make this boarding procedure REALLY complicated and emotionally tiring"
Tourists on my flight to Spain.

"Yay! We're flying a 767!" - no passenger, ever.

By the time your operations make it to Six Sigma - don't be surprised if demand has shifted to an entirely different product.

"There are no bad ideas in a creative workshop!" - "Except for the idea there are no bad ideas!" - Two facilitators caught in logic loop.

Looking for some statistics, or market research on whether socks *size* correlates to how much *luck* they bring. Big Data, please help.

Paradox: one hides lack of results behind frantic activity, but one celebrates results that require only few actions.

Creating KPI's for a new product and creating the product itself are very different, yet often confused activities. #1 is talk, #2 is real.

If your job implies using a lot of statistical tools, raise your credibility by admitting being wrong regularly. It's statistics.

2nd grumpy innovator

THE TWO JOBS *EVERY* CREATIVE ROLE HAS BEEN SPLIT INTO*

* Inspired by Wulff & Morgenthaler

The market research industry has a new way of mixing correlation and causation into happy BS aka "storytelling".

You will never have enough research for it to make the final decision for you. Ask yourself what the minimum is you need to keep moving.

"IF I CAN'T HAVE ANOTHER RUNWAY THEN I WANT MORE TERMINALS". Gatwick is what happens when you give in to airport planners' tantrums.

For market researchers, 95% confidence is good enough. Right up to the moment you ask them to invest their own cash in the project.

Something scary is happening in Operations teams everywhere, now that heuristics are being overruled by theory... Excellence Team, are you reciting business books or hands-on experience?

(Bureaucracy Impact) = (# Layers between you and any tangible effect of your decisions) / (# Decisions you make)

"Warp 10, captain? We'll have to wait for the FMEA team to report back first, sir."
Scotty, after TQM roll-out on Starship Enterprise.

"Captain, structural integrity is down to 18%"
Mr Spock halfway through Six-Sigma DMAIC and not liking where this is heading.

Hey UX people - well done on reframing User-Interface as User-Experience. But remember UX is still a means to an end, not an end in itself.

If decisions depend on nuances smaller than the measurements' margin of error, the decision making is the problem, not the measurements.

A Marketer walks into an on-premise, high-energy touch point, experiences a red/orange 2nd moment of truth and converts. <-- Jargon

When will architecture & civil engineering courses finally teach that white is not a filth & bird shit proof colour for buildings?

> **Calling it a 'reorganization' implies there was some level of organization to start with.**

Market research credibility is defined by the n (sample) and money spent ($). Both must be high, the rest seems to be irrelevant.

Note that in every segmentation study, one of the personas is the SPSS waste bin, the statistical equivalent of Quasimodo.

"USE IN CASE OF EMERGENCY ONLY"
What the label on my hotel room coffee brewer should have said, to manage my expectations.

Cleaning the data? You mean change your perception of reality to fit your model.

The most amazing part of the news that the NSA has been eavesdropping French government data, is that they managed to decipher Minitel OS.

Clusters. They come in bombs, computers, SPSS analysis, headaches and f-ups.

Do you need lots of data or is one good date enough?

> **The fact someone wrote a blog post about it doesn't necessarily make it true, nor a valuable piece of information.**

"Find correlation, imply causality" - the cynical reality of most Market Research. In desperation to show value, the industry achieves the opposite.

Hey Six Sigma Black Belt, are you as comfortable working through 1, 2, 3, 4 and 5 Sigma using axle grease and a ruler rather than Excel?

The Trend Watcher Algorithm:
ECHO($OtherTrendWatcher);END

The Strategy Consultant Algorithm: IF($Reality)≠($Forecast); CLAIM("Yes but"+RANDOM(NewsItem)
+"Not my fault);END.

High Purchase Intent scores? Be aware shoppers aren't even loyal to their own shopping list, before taking their answers too seriously.

The Data Paradox: the surge in volume of data generated globally is not from increased knowledge, but from being too lazy to be succinct.

Social media - where so many confuse being 'active' with 'productive'.

2nd grumpy innovator

**I CAN SEE IT'S A LIFE BOAT.
BUT IS IT SAFE?**

"To slay a monster, we had to create a monster" *Movie pitch for the first action movie about ISO9001.*

The more complex the rules are, the simpler they are to bend. And vice versa. Stage gates, innovation protocols, regulation, corporate bonuses.

Data is NOT like oxygen. No one chokes on oxygen.

You can be 100% certain that none of the brands shown in your trend report used any of the trends identified to set the trends. None.

Market Research Movies

The Shawshank Regression	Bridge On The River Quantile	$\alpha > 0.05$ About Mary
The Good, The Bad & The Outlier	Variable Independence Day	Monsters User Community
A Sample Plan	The Binomial Man	Sophie's Multiple Choice
World War Z-Test	Django Uncorrelated	N=1 In The West
American Histogram X	A Christmas Correlation	The $\alpha < 0.05$ Suspects
Top-1 Box Blood	Graph Of Thrones	Mean Squared Streets
The Wizard Of Odds	Nemo's Key Findings	When The Bell Curves
Specific Rim	The Averagers	Rebel Without Causality

"Real-time Big Data Analytics" anagrams to "Amicably Agitated Latrines". Just so you know what to say when you meet a specialist.

A concept benefit that is so abstract that it is impossible to disagree with, will reap high test scores but has no value in market.

Luck, Patience & Being Right

I SAW IT IN A DREAM.

Luck, Patience & Being Right

Optimists and Pessimists will both refer to themselves as Realists, which neither are. When it comes to innovation, the Realists are characterised by their comfort with ambiguity. Where the Optimist presumes all will be Sunny and speedy, the Pessimist counts on a dark and Murky path ahead.

The Realists openly admit they're not 100% sure about what's ahead, but welcome the choices and compromises that land on their path – *while they walk it* – en route to a good outcome. They are confident to trust their own judgment and that of their travel companions.

This is the essential characteristic of a great innovator, crucial for achieving success in Stretch and Game Changing innovation. Being comfortable to make big decisions, or even change course, when you're already on the way because you know it's beneficial to the objective.

This is *fundamentally* different from what is expected of managers in large corporate organisations. In these operational environments the norm is to lock in all the 'evidence' at the start, chart a map of the whole journey up front and not move before a certain 'objective' parameter has been met. As soon as things then deviate from the map, which they *always* will, all energy is then focused on updating the map and keeping everyone who agreed to that map on board instead of dealing with the new reality itself and perhaps revising the destination.

2nd grumpy innovator

When you're innovating to go into unknown territory, maps are always going to be incomplete[14]. Instead, bring a compass and course-correct when necessary.

Ambiguity seen through the lens of corporate management equals 'risk' and is inherently unwelcome. Which is why (at Happen) we call the people who can handle it well 'Rebels'. Their innate way of dealing with uncertainty goes against the grain of what the MBA-skewed norm requires, but it certainly raises the chances of success on the more radical end of the innovation spectrum.

Here's a nice visual from a Rebel friend on how the decision-making process differs. First the classic way of 'finding opportunity' in a business environment.

	category parameter 2					
NO	NO	NO	NO	NO	NO	NO
NO	NO	NO	NO	YES!	NO	NO
NO	NO	NO	NO	NO	NO	NO
NO	NO	NO	NO	NO	NO	NO
NO	YES!	NO	NO	NO	NO	NO
NO	NO	NO	NO	NO	NO	NO

(y-axis: category parameter 1; x-axis: category parameter 2)

- You chart the market along a number of parameters relevant to the category, ideally two so you can make nice graphs. In a food category, this could be as simple as 'time of day' and 'consumer demographic'.

---

[14] I have a hunch that more energy is spent on updating Gantt charts with hindsight than there is on scheduling up front.

- You spend time researching and validating each segment's business potential. This often involves quantitative research, asking consumers what they might need. The highest scoring segments pop out as what is worth pursuing with a Stretch or Game Changing innovation.

Now... This will all seem pretty solid at first glance and it certainly services the urge for rigour before diving in. But sadly, it's a false sense of security.

- The parameters by which you chart, are your own hypothetical ones and more likely to be business-led than by consumer need. It *appears* that you are charting a full map of the world. Even 'big data' doesn't provide patterns, only the confirmation of hypotheses you feed in.

- Any consumer research to further validate the chart is likely to be survey based and ask opinions on future, hypothetical situations. This means you're paying friendly people to answer surveys about situations they don't know yet.

Even more problematic: *it takes so much time*, which is the one scarce resource in mature competitive markets.

Then how do the Rebels do this? Well, I dare say *completely* differently. First of all, they start with a much less sharply scoped space to start from, at best an area of opportunity. In this fuzzy place, they start asking themselves (and their team) very simple questions (up/down, left/right, old/young, men/women, lunch/dinner) to *form an opinion* on what the opportunity really is.

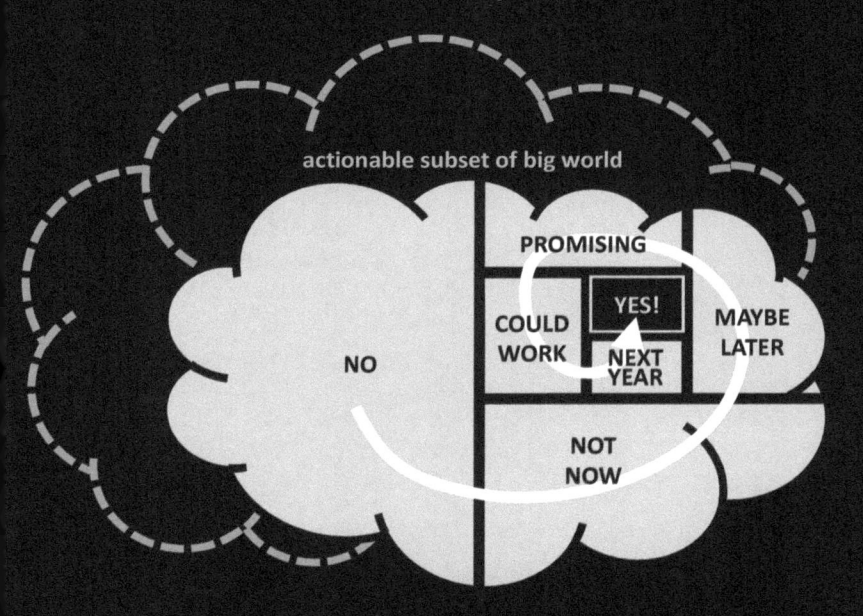

Rebels approach their innovation task much more iteratively, trusting their judgment on what will be the best next step. By this I do not mean they travel only on gut feel. By judgment I mean they are confident that when a fork in the road presents itself, they can decide then & there what information is required to make the right decision.

Why is the Rebellious, exploratory approach so powerful in Stretch and Game Changing innovation?

- Because you navigate iteratively towards a solution instead of parachuting down into one, you can always take a step back if your last decision turned out incorrect.

- You can start almost immmediately, you won't need to invest heavily up front in validation and — best of all — you need less steps in total.

- With less investment sunk in at the front end, you can walk away sooner and more easily if there turns out to be no business opportunity. Yes, *this* is what useful 'failing faster' looks like.

- No matter how virtually/realistically rigorous your upfront 'classic' investigation is... Because Stretch and Game Changing innovation imply moving away from your heartland: mistakes are made. The new territory is *never* like you imagined it and solutions will fail at first. Remember it's not just new for you, but for your consumer just as much.

Combine such an approach with a cross-functional, result oriented team from the previous chapters and you'll bring a bright future so much closer.

How to recognize the Rebels in your business?

You'll by now have made the link to the 'Personality-led' innovation I referred to in earlier chapters. Yes, these are the Rebels and you might now think this requires spotting the Bransons, Roddicks & Musks in your business at an early age.

Luckily it isn't.

As an agency working with the cream of innovators in mass consumer businesses, the past decade has given us insight and a surprising picture of what type of people consistently manage to define, develop and launch successful innovations. Winning streaks, not lucky strikes.

- **They know what luck looks like.** They are fully immersed in your business, have ears everywhere and are acutely aware when good vibes are in the air. Both in the market and inside the organisation.

- **They are patient.** It was a big surprise to us how so many of these Rebels are not at all the loud showmen & women we'd expected. Most are introverts. And because of their sharp sense of 'lucky' circumstances, they're fine to wait until market & organisational winds are favourable.

- **They know they're right.** They also know that when they are wrong, they'll *make* it right. That's different from pushing through an opion with a pig-headed mindset. It's *confidence*.

There you have it. Inside your business sit people who know where to look for the next promising innovation and they're patiently waiting for the right moment to act.

How to draw them out? The three characteristics on the previous page all come to the surface as *good judgment* of an opportunity.

When these people succeed once, they are likely to succeed again and again. *Acknowledge they were the success factor, not the system they operate in.*

They are attracted to the trickier ends of the innovation spectrum and the will find ways to cheat the system to make it work. In fact, they often *have to* cheat the system, which is designed for the operational end of the spectrum. *Allow them to.*

They are intrinsically motivated to innovate, which means they are more excited about results in market than being part of a particular group, brand or business. If their patience eventually runs out, they will go succeed elsewhere. *Give them space.*

The Rebels in your business are a prime case for successes in the past being your best guarantee for more success in the future. How to tap their value?

Simple: with **TRUST**.

But that's another book entirely.

2nd grumpy innovator

[**To get stuff done, it's better to have a simple process and great people, than a great process and simple people.**]

[biz bureaucracy level] = 1/[biz trust level]

So George Orwell got the date wrong for 1984 by about 25 years. Now, does that make him an optimist or a pessimist?

"Google stops Glass development for looking too dorky". Bluetooth headset users disagree.

It's somewhat unnerving when politicians mix up the terms "consumer" and "citizen".

"You want a proven methodology, but in a form totally customised to your situation, of course."
The management consultant's daily dilemma.

"Our product is so new, we're inventing a new word to describe it!"
Innovation team getting ready to add "positioning problem" to their to-do list.

"My raw cookie dough concept is just way ahead of its time!" Indeed, you should have kept it in the oven for at least another 15 minutes.

"How do you measure a concept's potential to surprise consumers?"
Tiptoe-box Score

"Stand back, this is going to make some noise!"
Introduction to what can only be an AMAZING prototype test.

Anthropomorphism: Human capability that shows
A) our incredible brainpower
B) flaw that gets us eaten by animals with big eyes

Asking for 5 years' experience in social media marketing is the same as looking for one of Mark Zuckerberg's first five team members.

> **Are you spreading your focus or being selectively focused? Not the same.**

That human tendency to translate "different" into either "better" or "worse", instead of just "different".

Great insight is less about looking for new things to see and more about new understanding of what you've been seeing all along.

Leadership vision can be myopic too.

> **Building relationships starts with giving, not taking. It's that simple.**

"What?! This sausage is only 8% real meat!? A disgrace!" - Someone ignorant of their pension being only 4% real money.

Only in hindsight are there wrong or right decisions. In real life, there are only wrong and "seems promising" ones.

Putting a * in front of your LinkedIn profile name will indeed ensure you come up tops in my phone's contact list. But not for very long.

> **I sold my hammer and bought a clipper instead. But every problem still looks like a nail.**

When Titans clash, fetch popcorn and wait until they're tired before stepping in.

The relevance of having 95% confidence in statistics-driven decisions depends entirely on the impact of the 5% chance of being wrong.

I suggest simplifying MBTI to two profiles when it comes to segmenting humans: Makers and Breakers.

Objective decision making? It's your neck on the line, not the data's. Use unbiased information for subjective decision making.

> **Don't go looking for 'objective' opinions. 'Unbiased' is a better angle.**

Once your track record gives you confidence to explain things simply, you forget how much detail your audience needs to learn the hard way.

You ALWAYS have more than one option. The other option being 'doing nothing', which also has its benefits & costs.

"Opportunity" is an actionable subset of what's happening around you.

> **Anyone claiming a child-like mind-set is good for innovation clearly hasn't spent much time around children.**

100% Focus implies 0% attention to the areas where the unexpected events might help/hamper your initiative. Allow your mind to wander

The difference between an error and a crisis is the solution coming from reversing or forwarding the time line.

Coffee cup lids. Why do coffee shop baristas insist "because of safety", yet airline stewards not bother? I agree with the airlines btw.

> **If you've just suffered a marketing disaster, more marketing is probably not going to get you out of trouble.**

Hey CEO, the shelves your country MD is showing you on the shop tour look impeccable, that's because they cleaned them just before you came.

That trend report you're about to buy is probably more expensive than flying over and having a look for yourself.

Mountaineering: you want gear that is lightweight, unbreakable, waterproof and that you can sleep in. Like a simpler version of business travel gear.

It's the project post-mortem meeting that actually kills the idea beyond rescue, not the actions before. There is always a solution.

When your day's calendar looks like a Tetris screen, unleash the Space Invaders.

Maritime wisdom: you must step UP into a lifeboat. That's a metaphor for countless things in life.

You only live once - and so do the friends, family and partners who choose to spend their time with you. Don't waste their time, be nice.

At what age do you shift from trying to make your parents proud of you, to trying to make your kids proud of you?

For most brand gurus, everything tangible that doesn't comply top-down to their genius vision is a nuisance to step on.

I totally believe Google's self-driving car can handle Californian traffic. But I'm not convinced until I see it take on Naples.

**HE GOT UP THERE WHILE WE WERE STILL PLANNING.
LET'S REPORT BACK WE FOUND A SAFE ROUTE GUARANTEEING AT LEAST SECOND PLACE.**

2nd grumpy innovator

Poolry ecuxeted idaes tedn to annyo poeple. No mratte how gdoo hte idae is.

The time of year that 95% of Americans forget that 95% of the Planet do not celebrate Thanksgiving.

Set ambitions, not as end goal but as reference framework to judge how well you're doing.

"I will also use this picture as my LinkedIn mugshot." *How many people brief their wedding photographer.*

I AGREE OUR BUSINESS PLAN IS THIN. BUT WE DO HAVE PING PONG *AND* AIR HOCKEY TABLES CRAMMED INTO OUR OFFICE.

I am a mixed-blood international entrepreneur.
Does that make me multicultural or border-agnostic?

Suddenly, I wonder why base jumpers even bother wearing a helmet.
Probably because their moms insist.

A 1-letter typo can make the difference between using and suing your regulatory audit team.

"Better to return halfway, than ending up lost completely" - Dutch proverb. Good stuff, those Dutch proverbs.

On a QWERTY keyboard, mis-aligning your right hand when starting an email with 'HI!' can lead to 'JO!' (good) or 'FU!' (not good).

⎡ **True independence is not expressed in "money in bank" but "daytime naps per week".** ⎤

To everyone who is about to turn 40. That's the age you can no longer be a 'high potential' and you have to start delivering the goods, FYI.

Step 1 in improving efficiency is building *trust*, not process control. Simply because it allows you to scrap meetings and reviews.

I can confirm that one downside of passing the age of 40 is that all your face's sweat glands migrate to your upper lip.

Contracts and signed agreements: if they are written properly, they can stay tucked away in the drawer forever.

If your first business value is "simplicity", I think having six more values on your list is pushing the definition a little.

I wonder how many EU politicians are truly aware that its economic, trade focused origins are what prevented wars, not its politics.

> **Hey Entrepreneur, ask not how to grow the business. Ask how to stop getting in the way of it growing itself.**

Has anyone ever explored a correlation between Lego-or-Playmobil childhood, MSDos-or-MacOS teens and a Windows-or-iOS adulthood?

I have a hunch that successful artists are in fact successful businesspeople with an artsy hobby to fill the gaps between deals.

Youths' frontal lobes & planning ability don't mature until their 25th. Remember that when you ask them about their purchase intent in market research.

New metropolitan metric: UDOSOPK(x) aka Unsolicited-Drugs-Or-Sex-Offers-Per-Kilometer.
NYC: 0.2. Ams: 1. Paris: 0.5 Tokyo: 0.01. Shanghai: 5.

"I don't know" and "I don't care".
Correlation, causation, inverse-correlation, inverse-causality, or all of the previous? Discuss.

Hiring one CEO for $50m or two for $20m each. What's the better deal?

My shredder has just died halfway through processing my Xmas clean-up. I'm now wondering if the other half is really that confidential.

Frequent flyer dilemma. You're in biz class, your colleague in coach. Do you walk over and bring
A] Newspaper
B] Champagne
C] Smug looks

I can confirm eating sage is good for memory. I now remember I didn't like the taste of sage in my food.

I wonder if Amazon's suggestion engine eventually becomes so good, it suggests that one perfect book after which you're done reading.

[Pick my brain? What are you, a zombie?]

Planes, Trains & Automobiles.
BUT FOR GOD'S SAKE NO BUSSES PLEASE.

The only true entrepreneurial incentive for your employees isn't a big bonus upon success - it's taking away their house upon failure.

"Sophisticated" and "Complicated" are not synonyms. If anything, they're antonyms.

Serial Entrepreneur aka ADHD Entrepreneur.

I have a T-shaped consultant's shirt.

> **If you don't like the facts, then 'denial' is a great short term tactic.**

Hey creative guru, please plan your workshop out-of-the-box-thinking activities such that they only curl one toe at a time.

Successful entrepreneurship is less about delivering punches and much more about evading them with the occasional smack on the nose.

I prefer coffee froth over frothing coughs.

"YOU MEAN YOU LOST THE GOODS?!"
Fun thing to yell to your travel companion after you pass the airport sniffer dogs.

There are 2 types of developers. One believes anything outside their own expertise is simple.
The other empathises *all* development is complex.

Our new training program "Dealing with OCD" will start Monday or Tuesday, or maybe next week.
9am-ish, address TBC and no need to worry!

Product designers persistently present subjective opinions as objective facts.
At least fashion designers don't pretend.

Is Wednesday too early in the week to wish someone a nice weekend?

When "Genau!" just doesn't cut it, say "Wahnsinn!"
German lessons for beginners like me.

I knew London Luton Airport was nowhere near London. I found Luton Airport Station is nowhere near Luton Airport either. Luton, you liar :-(

Make sure you have its business card, before the opportunity walks off into the sunset.

When you agree something via video conference, aka "screen resolution".

> **You only live once. And so do the friends, family and partners who choose to spend their time with you. Don't waste their time, be nice.**

"It wasn't me"
Opening line in all IT support calls and project review meetings.

Just had haircut, cut off enough hair to fill a pillow. But that's gross, so I'm selling it to a taxidermist.

Scientific approach to being an entrepreneur?
You mean you're setting up a separate 2nd business as double blind control group to disprove your hypothesis? Yeah right.

There's no such thing as "late". Only "too late", because everything else is clearly "on time enough".

If you observe poorly, you lose connection to the world around you. If you listen poorly, you lose connection to the people around you.

The Wise man knows when to shut up. The Leader knows when to shut someone else up.

You need a LOT of theory to dislodge heuristic behaviours. And that's for a good reason.

[**Do not mistake indifference for tolerance.**]

SU ~~MO~~NDAY

YOU ARE NOW ALL INSTRUCTED TO BE MORE ENTREPRENEURIAL!

*** SPOILER ALERT ***
Experience *does* matter.
But you only learn that from experience.

My attempt to spice up my stroll to the gate with some Urban Parkour free-running is not being appreciated by airport security. :-(

Totally relaxed or total loss of decorum?

Cash flow is real, profit merely an opinion.

Using only one data source to claim you're right is only allowed if that source is your gut.

I'm in Dusseldorf. Which I had to explain to my kids is not from Harry Potter.

"Everyone always takes credit for my success."
Luck

Getting dirty is part of the game in any business; the question is if the dirt is gathering IN you or ON you.

If you insist on digging for a "reason why" for everything, then brace yourself for uncovering some incredibly banal ones.

> **Long term success is only granted to the few who manage to convert lucky strikes into winning streaks.**

If you don't have this one already ...

Order one now. I hear it's funny.

Premise of the 1st Grumpy Book

Anyone celebrating the tenacity of successful innovators is probably ignoring the far larger number of tenacious idiots pursuing bad ideas. If you think about the classic description of what character traits help people succeed in turning an innovative idea into a profitable business stream – winners and losers at this particular game are frighteningly similar:

- *Dogged determination*
- *Blind devotion to their idea*
- *Unshakable confidence, against all odds*

There must be a fine line between getting it very right or very wrong. In fact, I think there's a paradox hidden in there.

Companies are structured entities, with defined procedures and efficient processes that ensure things get done. Even the messiest of businesses are organized to some level. In stark contrast, the *reality* they operate in is unpredictable, fluid, ugly and most of all: immense. In this simple contrast lies a beautiful paradox: it is the reason there will always be new opportunities & needs for new things *and* it is the main reason for failing at successfully doing so. The attributes that guarantee new opportunities are the opposite of what an efficient corporate system thrives upon.

The chart on the next page shows how the four capabilities crucial to running a business are hampered in the context of innovation[15]. Within the neatly controlled corporate

---

[15] *Yes, you can slice business up many other ways too. But this particular way happens to work well for my story.*

ecosystem, they do as they're asked to and all is fine – as long as they keep looking inward.

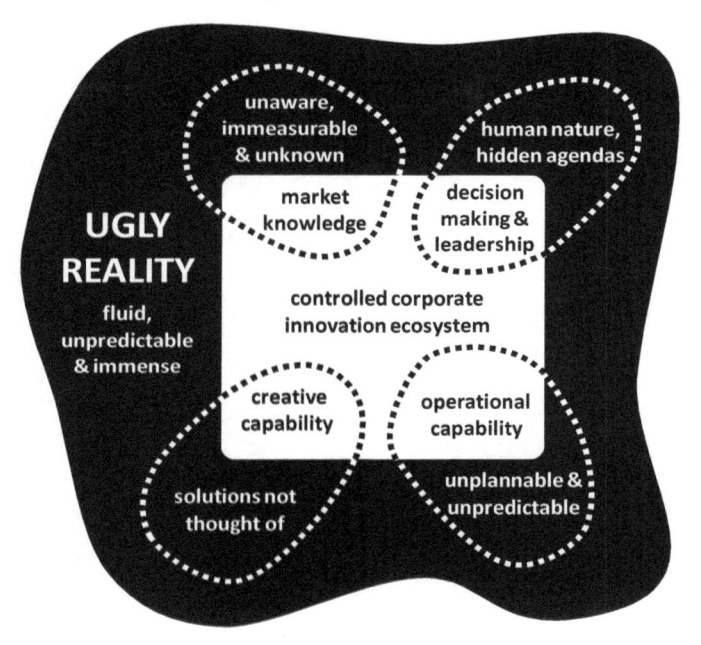

UGLY REALITY
fluid, unpredictable & immense

- unaware, immeasurable & unknown — market knowledge
- human nature, hidden agendas — decision making & leadership
- controlled corporate innovation ecosystem
- solutions not thought of — creative capability
- unplannable & unpredictable — operational capability

I've found most of the failures in innovation can be brought back to individuals and teams in denial of the reality outside of their campus walls, totally unnecessarily.

This little book holds some of the thoughts I had seeing this happen. If you have experience in the innovation arena, you may recognize attitudes, situations and odd behaviours. Don't worry, we'll keep those our little secret.

Further salutations

A big THANK YOU to my fellow founders and our incredible teams at Happen & Winkle, you are the reason I get out of bed in the morning. Albeit only if I'm not out of bed already for being with my wife and children first.

Another big THANK YOU to all the client teams who not only challenge us daily with delightful innovation questions, but also laugh with us about the peculiarities this work often brings.

Warm and bountiful THANK YOU's to the Rebels who come to Happen's Rebel events — you know who you are — this book wouldn't exist without you. You're probably holding a free copy in your hands now.

And THANK YOU anonymous reader of this book.
I hope it made you smile, it was a pleasure writing. Get in touch to let me know your thoughts, your messages are very welcome.

Thank you all,

Costas Papaikonomou

Twitter: @grumpyinnovator
Email: costas@grumpyinnovator.com

Printed in Poland
by Amazon Fulfillment
Poland Sp. z o.o., Wrocław